EX LIBRIS

VINTAGE CLASSICS

TOUCHING THE VOID

Joe Simpson is the author of several best-selling books, of which the first, *Touching the Void*, won both the NCR Award and the Boardman Tasker Award. His later books are *This Game of Ghosts*, *Storms of Silence*, *Dark Shadows Falling*, *The Beckoning Silence* and a novel, *The Water People*.

OTHER WORKS BY JOE SIMPSON

The Water People
(A Novel)
This Game of Ghosts
Storms of Silence
Dark Shadows Falling
The Beckoning Silence

JOE SIMPSON

Touching the Void

WITH A FOREWORD BY
Chris Bonington

VINTAGE BOOKS
London

Published by Vintage 1997

3 5 7 9 10 8 6 4

Copyright © Joe Simpson 1988

The right of Joe Simpson to be identified as the author of this work
has been asserted by him in accordance with the Copyright,
Designs and Patents Act, 1988

First published in Great Britain in 1988 by Jonathan Cape

Vintage
Random House, 20 Vauxhall Bridge Road,
London SW1V 2SA

www.vintage-classics.info

Addresses for companies within The Random House Group Limited
can be found at: www.randomhouse.co.uk/offices.htm

The Random House Group Limited Reg. No. 954009

A CIP catalogue record for this book
is available from the British Library

ISBN 9780099511748

The Random House Group Limited supports The Forest
Stewardship Council (FSC), the leading international forest
certification organisation. All our titles that are printed on
Greenpeace approved FSC certified paper carry the FSC logo.
Our paper procurement policy can be found at:
www.rbooks.co.uk/environment

Printed and bound in Great Britain by
CPI Cox & Wyman, Reading, RG1 8EX

To
SIMON YATES
for a debt I can never repay

And to those friends who have gone to the mountains
and have not returned

Contents

FOREWORD
by Chris Bonington

I first met Joe in Chamonix last winter. Like many climbers he had decided it was time to learn to ski, had no intention of taking formal lessons and was teaching himself. I had heard and read stories about him, of desperately narrow escapes on the mountains, particularly his latest escapade in Peru, but they had made only a limited impact.

Sitting beside him in a bar in Chamonix it was difficult putting the stories and reputation to the person. He was dark, with a slightly punk hairstyle, and there was something abrasive in his manner. I found it difficult to take him in my mind from the streets of Sheffield into the mountains. And I didn't think much more about him until I read the manuscript of *Touching the Void*. It wasn't just the remarkable nature of the story – and it was remarkable, one of the most incredible stories of survival that I have ever read – it was the quality of the writing that was both sensitive and dramatic, capturing the extremes of fear, suffering and emotion both of himself and his partner, Simon Yates. From the moment Joe slipped and fell, breaking his leg on the descent, through his solitary agony in the crevasse until the moment he crawled into their base camp, I was riveted, unable to put the book down.

To put Joe's struggle for survival in perspective, I can compare it to my own experience on the Ogre in 1977, when Doug Scott slipped whilst abseiling from the summit and broke both legs. At this stage the situation was similar to the early part of Joe's ordeal. There were just two of us near the top of a particularly inhospitable mountain. But for us there were two other team members in a snow cave on the col just below the summit block. We were caught by a storm and took six days, five of them without food, to get down. On the way I slipped and broke my ribs. It was the worst experience I have ever had in the mountains and yet, compared to what Joe Simpson went through on his own, it begins to pale.

A close parallel happened on Haramosh in the Karakoram in 1957. It was an Oxford University party trying to make the first ascent of this 24,270 foot peak. They had just decided to turn back; two of the members, Bernard Jillot and John Emery, wanted to go just a little farther on the ridge to get photographs and were swept away in a wind slab avalanche. They survived the fall and their team mates went down to rescue them, but this was only the start of a long-drawn-out catastrophe, from which only two emerged alive.

Theirs, too, was an intriguing and very moving story but it was told by a professional writer and, because of this, lacks the immediacy and strength of someone writing at first hand. This is where Joe Simpson scores. Not only is it one of the most incredible survival stories of which I have heard, it is superbly and poignantly told and deserves to become a classic in this genre.

February 1988

All men dream: but not equally.
Those who dream by night in the dusty
recesses of their minds wake in the day
to find that it was vanity: but the dreamers
of the day are dangerous men, for they may
act their dreams with open eyes, to make it
possible.

  T.E. Lawrence, *The Seven Pillars of Wisdom*

KEY
1 1st snow hole
2 2nd snow hole
3 3rd snow hole
4 4th snow hole
A Accident site
X Rope cut
C Cliff and crevasse
a 1st snow hole on crawl
b 2nd night alone
B Bomb alley
---- Ascent & lowers

The crawl-out from the face

I

BENEATH THE MOUNTAIN LAKES

I was lying in my sleeping bag, staring at the light filtering through the red and green fabric of the dome tent. Simon was snoring loudly, occasionally twitching in his dream world. We could have been anywhere. There is a peculiar anonymity about being in tents. Once the zip is closed and the outside world barred from sight, all sense of location disappears. Scotland, the French Alps, the Karakoram, it was always the same. The sounds of rustling, of fabric flapping in the wind, or of rainfall, the feel of hard lumps under the ground sheet, the smell of rancid socks and sweat – these are universals, as comforting as the warmth of the down sleeping bag.

Outside, in a lightening sky, the peaks would be catching the first of the morning sun, with perhaps even a condor cresting the thermals above the tent. That wasn't too fanciful either since I had seen one circling the camp the previous afternoon. We were in the middle of the Cordillera Huayhuash, in the Peruvian Andes, separated from the nearest village by twenty-eight miles of rough walking, and surrounded by the most spectacular ring of ice mountains I had ever seen, and the only indication of this from within our tent was the regular roaring of avalanches falling off Cerro Sarapo.

I felt a homely affection for the warm security of the tent, and reluctantly wormed out of my bag to face the prospect of lighting the stove. It had snowed a little during the night, and the grass crunched frostily under my feet as I padded over to the cooking rock. There was no sign of Richard stirring as I

15

passed his tiny one-man tent, half collapsed and whitened with hoar frost.

Squatting under the lee of the huge overhanging boulder that had become our kitchen, I relished this moment when I could be entirely alone. I fiddled with the petrol stove which was mulishly objecting to both the temperature and the rusty petrol with which I had filled it. I resorted to brutal coercion when coaxing failed and sat it atop a propane gas stove going full blast. It burst into vigorous life, spluttering out two-foot-high flames in petulant revolt against the dirty petrol.

As the pan of water slowly heated, I looked around at the wide, dry and rock-strewn river bed, the erratic boulder under which I crouched marking the site at a distance in all but the very worst weather. A huge, almost vertical wall of ice and snow soared upwards to the summit of Cerro Sarapo directly in front of the camp, no more than a mile and a half away. Rising from the sea of moraine to my left, two spectacular and extravagant castles of sugar icing, Yerupaja and Rasac, dominated the camp site. The majestic 21,000-foot Siula Grande lay behind Sarapo and was not visible. It had been climbed for the first time in 1936 by two bold Germans via the North Ridge. There had been few ascents since then, and the true prize, the daunting 4,500-foot West Face had so far defeated all attempts.

I turned off the stove and gingerly slopped the water into three large mugs. The sun hadn't cleared the ridge of mountains opposite and it was still chilly in the shadows.

'There's a brew ready, if you're still alive in there,' I announced cheerfully.

I gave Richard's tent a good kicking to knock off the frost and he crawled out looking cramped and cold. Without a word he headed straight for the river bed, clutching a roll of toilet paper.

'Are you still bad?' I asked when he returned.

'Well, I'm not the full ticket but I reckon I'm over the worst. It was bloody freezing last night.'

I wondered if it was the altitude rather than the kidney-bean stew that was getting to him. Our tents were pitched at 15,000 feet, and he was no mountaineer.

Simon and I had found Richard resting in a sleazy hotel in Lima, halfway through his six-month exploration of South America. His wire-rimmed glasses, neat practical clothing and bird-like mannerisms hid a dry humour and a wild repertoire of beachcombing reminiscences. He had lived off grubs and berries with pygmies while dug-out canoeing through the rain forests of Zaire, and had watched a shoplifter being kicked to death in a Nairobi market. His travelling companion was shot dead by trigger-happy soldiers in Uganda for no more than a dubious exchange of cassette tapes.

He travelled the world between bouts of hard work to raise funds. Usually he journeyed alone to see where chance encounters in alien countries would take him. There were distinct advantages, we thought, to having an entertaining watchman in camp to keep an eye on the gear while Simon and I were out climbing. It was probably a gross injustice to the poor hill farmers in this remote spot, but in the backstreets of Lima we had become suspicious of everyone. Anyway, we had invited Richard to come up and join us for a few days if he wanted to see the Andes at close quarters.

It had been two days' walk from where the bone-shaking bus deposited us after 80 heart-stopping miles up the mountain valleys. Forty-six people were crammed into a ramshackle vehicle designed to carry twenty-two, and we were not fortified by the sight of so many wayside shrines to dead bus drivers and their passengers. The engine was held together with nylon string and a flat tyre was changed with a pick-axe.

By the end of the second day, Richard was feeling the effects of altitude. Dusk was gathering as we approached the head of the valley, and he urged Simon and me to go ahead with the donkeys and prepare camp before dark; he would take his time to follow. The way was straightforward now – he couldn't go wrong, he had said.

Slowly he staggered up the treacherous moraines to the lake where he thought we were camped and then remembered a second lake on the map. It had begun to rain and grew increasingly cold. A thin shirt and light cotton trousers were poor protection from a chill Andean night. Tired out, he had descended to the valley in search of shelter. On the way up he had noticed some dilapidated stone and corrugated-iron huts which he assumed to be empty but sufficiently sheltered for a night's rest. He was surprised to find them occupied by two teenage girls and a large brood of children.

After protracted negotiation, he managed to get a place to sleep in the adjoining pigsty. They gave him some boiled potatoes and cheese to eat, and threw in a bundle of moth-eaten sheepskins for warmth. It was a long cold night, and the high-altitude lice enjoyed their best feed for a long time.

Simon came over to the cooking rock and regaled us with a vivid dream. He was firmly convinced that these weird hallucinations were a direct result of the sleeping pills he was taking. I resolved to try some that very night.

I swallowed the last of my coffee as Simon took control of the breakfast-making and then started to write in my diary:

19 May 1985. Base camp. Heavy frost last night, clear skies this morning. I'm still trying to adjust to being here. It feels menacingly remote and exhilarating at the same time; so much better than the Alps – no hordes of climbers, no helicopters, no rescue – just us and the mountains . . . Life seems far simpler and more real here. It's easy to let events and emotions flow past without stopping to look . . .

I wondered how much of this I really believed, and how it related to what we were doing in the Andes. Tomorrow we would start an acclimatisation climb up Rosario Norte. If fit enough at the end of ten days, we would attempt the unclimbed West Face of Siula Grande.

Simon handed me a bowl of porridge and more coffee:

'Shall we go tomorrow then?'

'Might as well. I can't see that it will take us very long if we go light. Could be back down by early afternoon.'

'My only worry is this weather. I'm not sure what it means.'

It had been the same every day since our arrival. The mornings would dawn fine and clear, but by midday banks of cumulus would move in from the east, followed by the inevitable rain. On the high slopes this came as heavy snowfall, and the risk of avalanches and lines of retreat cut off would suddenly become a reality. When such clouds massed in the Alps, retreat was always instantly considered. These weather patterns were different somehow.

'You know, I don't reckon it's anything like as bad as it seems,' Simon suggested thoughtfully. 'Look at yesterday. It clouded in and snowed, but the temperature didn't fall dramatically, there was no lightning or thunder, and there didn't appear to be any desperately high winds on the summits. I don't think these are storms at all.'

Simon could be right, but something was nagging at me, making me question him. 'Are you suggesting we should just climb on through a snowfall? If we do that, won't we run the risk of mistaking a serious storm for the normal pattern?'

'Well, yes, that is a risk. We'll just have to see how it goes. We're certainly not going to learn anything by sitting down here all the time.'

'Right! I was just being cautious about avalanches, that's all.'

Simon laughed. 'Yeah, well, you have good reason to be. Still you survived the last one. I reckon it will be more like the Alps in winter, all powder snow and spindrift, and no big wet snow avalanches. We'll just have to see.'

I envied Simon his carefree take-it-as-it-comes attitude. He had the force to take what was his for the taking, and the freedom of spirit to enjoy it without grumbling worries and doubts. He laughed more often than he grimaced, grinning at his own misfortune as readily as he did at other people's. Tall and powerfully built, he possessed most of life's advantages and few of the drawbacks. He was an easy friend: dependable, sincere, ready to see life as a joke. He had a thatch of blond hair, blue, blue laughing eyes, and that touch of madness which makes just a few people so special. I was glad that we had chosen to come here as a two-man team. There were few other people I could have coped with for so long. Simon was everything that I was not, everything I would like to have been.

'What time do you reckon you'll be back?' Richard asked dozily from his sleeping bag as Simon and I prepared to set off next morning.

'Three o'clock at the latest. We're not intending to spend long over it, and certainly not if the weather breaks again.'

'Okay. Good luck.'

The early-morning frost had hardened the loose ground and the going was easier than we anticipated. It wasn't long before we fell into a steady silent rhythm, zigzagging steadily up the screes. The tents became smaller each time I glanced back, and I began to enjoy the exercise, feeling fitter and stronger than I had thought I would. We were making fast progress despite the altitude, and Simon was keeping to a steady pace that matched mine. I had worried unduly about whether there would be a marked difference between us. If a climber has to slow his natural pace to that of his companion, the unfit climber will soon find himself struggling to keep up. I could imagine the frustrations and tensions that would arise from such a situation.

'How's it going?' I asked when we paused for a short rest.

'I feel pretty good, but I'm glad we're not smoking on this trip.'

I silently agreed, despite all my earlier protests at Simon's suggestion that we should take no cigarettes to base camp. I could feel my lungs working hard in the thin cold air. Heavy smoking had never affected my performance in the Alps, but I was forced to agree that it might be wise to stop during this expedition. The risks of high-altitude sickness and pulmonary oedemas, about which we had heard so much, were all that helped me through a rough few days craving tobacco.

It took a couple of hours to put the scree slopes behind us. Then we headed north towards a high col above an area of broken rock buttresses. The camp disappeared from view and immediately I became aware of the silence and the solitude of our position. For the first time in my life I knew what it meant to be isolated from people and society. It was wonderfully calming and tranquil to be here. I became aware of a feeling of complete freedom – to do what I wanted to do when I wanted to, and in whatever manner. Suddenly the whole day had changed. All lethargy was swept away by an invigorating independence. We had responsibilities to no one but ourselves now, and there would be no one to intrude or come to our rescue . . .

Simon was some distance ahead, quietly climbing, steadily gaining ground. Although he had stolen a march on my less methodical pace, I was no longer concerned about speed and fitness since I knew now that we were pretty evenly matched. I was not in any hurry, and knew we could both reach the summit easily. If a fine viewing point presented itself, I was happy to stop for a moment to take in the view.

The rocky gullies were loose and crumbling. As I emerged from behind a yellow outcrop, I was pleased to see Simon settled down on a col a couple of hundred feet away preparing a hot drink.

'The loose stuff wasn't as bad as I thought it was going to be,' I said a little breathlessly. 'But I could do with that brew.'

'Seen Siula Grande, just over there, left of Sarapo?'

'God, it's fantastic.' I was a little awed by the sight in front of me. 'It's far bigger than those photographs suggested.'

Simon handed me a steaming mug as I sat on my rucksack and gazed at the whole range laid out before us. To my left I could see the South Face of Rasac, a sweeping ice slope with rock bands crossing it, giving it a sort of stripy marbled effect. To the right of Rasac's snowy summit, and connected to it by a dangerously corniced ridge, I could see the slightly lower summit of Seria Norte. From there the corniced ridge dipped down to a saddle before curving up in a huge sweep over two shoulders of rock to the final summit pyramid of Yerupaja. It was by far the highest mountain to be seen and dominated our view as it reared, glistening with ice and fresh snow, high above the Siula glacier. Its South Face formed the classic triangular mountain shape; the West Ridge, corniced and rocky, arched up from the col below Seria Norte, the East Ridge curling round and dropping towards another col. The face below this ridge was an astonishing series of parallel powder-snow flutings etched like lace ribbons in the shadows cast by the sun.

At the base of the ridge I recognised the Santa Rosa col which we had seen in our photographs of Siula Grande. It formed the junction between Yerupaja's South-East Ridge and the start of Siula Grande's North Ridge. This ridge looked relatively uncomplicated where it began to climb up before narrowing and twisting in frighteningly thin edges of snowy cornice and flutings which hung precariously over the edge of the huge West Face. It peaked on the huge snow mushroom that formed the summit of Siula Grande.

That West Face was our ambition. At first it looked confusing, as if I hadn't seen it before. The scale, and the fact that I was looking at it from a different angle from that shown in the photographs, made it unrecognisable until gradually distinctive features fell into place. A huge bank of cumulus was beginning to spill up over the North Ridge of Siula Grande, as always moving in from the east where the huge rain forests of the Amazon basin, heated up in the day's sun, pushed out these regular banks of moisture-laden clouds.

'I think you're right about the weather, Simon,' I said. 'That's not storm weather at all. I'll bet it's just a convection system coming off the jungle.'

'Yeah, just getting up our normal afternoon dousing.'

'How high do you think we are now?' I asked.

'Must be about 18,000 feet, perhaps a bit more. Why?'

'Well, it's a height record for both of us, and we seem hardly to have noticed.'

'When you're sleeping at about the same height as Mont Blanc it doesn't seem very significant, does it?' Simon said with a mischievous grin.

By the time we had finished our drinks the first wet snowflakes were beginning to fall. The summit of Rosario was still clear, though it wouldn't be for very much longer. It was probably no more than 400 feet higher than our position on the col, and in clear weather could have been reached in little over an hour. Neither of us said anything about going straight down. It was an unspoken understanding between us that the summit would be left out this time.

Simon shouldered his pack and set off down towards the top of the scree slopes. He began to run and slide down the rocky gullies we had struggled up. Then we whooped and howled our way headlong down 1,500 feet of loose sliding screes, attempting to execute boots-together ski-turns, and arrived back at camp exhilarated and panting.

Richard had started to prepare the evening meal and handed us the mugs of tea he had made when he spotted us high on the screes. We sat by the roaring petrol stoves to tell him in rambling excited bursts what we had done and seen, until the rain came on up the valley in sudden waves and drove us into the shelter of the large dome tent.

After it grew dark at about six-thirty, anyone approaching the tent would have seen only a warm candlelight glowing red and green through the tent fabric and heard a quiet murmuring of conversation, punctuated now and then by gusts of ribald laughter as Richard told a hilarious story about eight members of a New Zealand rugby team lost in the jungles of central Africa. We planned our future training climbs before playing cards long into the night.

Our next objective was to be the unclimbed South Ridge of Cerro Yantauri, only a short walk across the river bed from our tents. Indeed it looked as if we would be in sight of camp all the way to the summit. The South Ridge ran from right to left up early rocky outcrops before forming a long and elegant corniced snow ridge which led to a highly unstable area of seracs that mushroomed to the summit. We would bivouac high on the ridge, either on the way up or on the descent, to test out our theories about the weather.

The morning was cold and sunny, but an unusually menacing look in the sky in the east persuaded us to leave the South Ridge of Yantauri for another day. Simon went for a bath and shave in a near-by ice-melt pool while I set off with Richard to see whether we could buy milk and cheese from the girls at the huts.

They seemed pleased to see us and were delighted to sell us their homemade cheese. Through Richard's halting Spanish, we discovered that their names were Gloria and Norma, and that they slept in the huts when they brought their father's cattle up to the high pastures. They had a wild, abandoned look about them, but they took great care of the little children, who seemed perfectly well able to look after themselves. We idled in the sun, watching them at work. Three-year-old Alecia (whom I had nicknamed Paddington) guarded the entrance to the cattle enclosure, preventing the cows and calves from escaping, while her brothers and sisters milked, or held back the calves from suckling, or prepared the whey in muslin bags. Everything was done with laughter at an unhurried happy pace. We arranged for Gloria's brother Spinoza to bring us supplies from the nearest village in the next few days and returned to camp nibbling on the cheese, keeping a wary eye on the clouds, which were about to empty their loads earlier than usual. The prospect of fresh vegetables, eggs, bread and fruit was almost too much to contemplate after two weeks on a monotonous diet of pasta and beans.

The next day we left the camp early for Yantauri. It was an inauspicious start. The screes proved highly dangerous, with stone-falls smacking down on them from high on the rubble-strewn West Face above us. We were nervous and jittery, and wanted to move fast, but our heavy sacks dictated otherwise. Half-way up the lower screes Simon realised he had left his camera down where he had last rested. He dumped his sack and ran back down while I carried on upwards to the right, heading for the protection of the lower rock walls.

By six o'clock that evening we were established high on the ridge, but the weather had taken a turn for the worse and dark threatening clouds were rapidly converging on our exposed position. As darkness fell we erected our little bivi tent against a small sheltered rock wall and settled down anxiously to sleep. It snowed steadily through the night but the feared storm did not materialise. Our weather theory seemed to be borne out.

We started up the snowy South Ridge in high hopes next morning, but at 18,000 feet we were forced to give up the struggle. Waist-deep powder snow had reduced us to an exhausted wallowing. The heavily corniced ridge would be far too dangerous. When I plunged through a fissure splitting a double cornice below the summit seracs and could see clear down the West Face we decided to call it a day.

Tired out, we returned to the tents after a trying descent of the loose rubble-strewn walls of the West Face. At least now we had some vital answers about the weather. Doubtless there would be serious storms at times, but at least we wouldn't have to retreat at the first sign of cloud build-up.

Two days later we set off again, this time for the South Ridge of Seria Norte. It looked spectacular from base camp, and as far as we knew it had never been climbed. As we drew closer we began to see why. Back home in Sheffield Al Rouse had told us that this was 'a ridge of some difficulty'. On close inspection we realised that Al's reputation for understatement was wholly justified. After a cold and cramped bivouac, we again sloughed up exhausting powder snow to reach a high col at the foot of the ridge. An astonishing series of cornices protruding almost vertically from the ridge leapfrogged 2,000 feet above us to the summit. To have touched the bottom cornice with an ice axe would have brought the whole mass of tottering ice tumbling down on to our heads. We managed to laugh at the waste of effort and wondered what Richard would think of our third failure to reach a summit. But we were fit, acclimatised and ready now for our main objective – the West Face of Siula Grande.

For two whole days we gorged ourselves on food and sunshine, preparing for the West Face. I began to feel spasms of fear now that we were committed to Siula in the next fine-weather window. What if something went wrong? It wouldn't take much to kill us off. I saw how very much alone we had chosen to be and felt small. Simon chuckled when I mentioned my worries. He knew the cause, and probably felt the same tension inside. It was healthy to be a little scared, and good to sense my body responding to the fear. We can do it, we can do it ... I kept repeating like a mantra whenever I felt that hollow hungry gap in my stomach. It wasn't false bravado. Psyching up for it, getting ready to make the final move, was always a difficult part of preparation for me. Rationalisation, some people called it – bloody frightened seemed a better description, and more honest!

'Okay,' Simon said finally, 'we snow-hole at the foot of the face, then go in one push the next day. Two days up, two days down, I reckon.'

'If the weather holds ...'

In the morning the outlook was bleak. Clouds hid the peaks and only their flanks were visible beneath a murky ceiling. There was an odd sense of menace in the air. We both noticed it as we packed our rucksacks in readiness for an early start the following day should the weather change. Was this to be a full-bore storm or simply an earlier than usual present from the Amazon? I pushed an extra cylinder of gas into my sack.

'I wouldn't mind winning the next one. So far it's mountains three, climbers nil.'

I smiled at Simon's rueful expression.

'It'll be different on Siula. For a start it's too bloody steep to hold much powder.'

'Four days you reckon, then,' Richard repeated casually.

'Five at the outside' – Simon glanced at me – 'and if we're not back after a week you'll be the proud owner of all our gear!'

I could see that Richard laughed only because we laughed. I didn't envy him the wait, never knowing what might be happening up there. Five days is a very long time, especially on your own with no one to talk to.

'You'll probably be jumping to all sorts of conclusions after three days, but try not to worry. We know what we're doing, and if something goes wrong there is nothing whatever you can do.'

Despite all our efforts to cut down on weight, the rucksacks were going to be a heavy burden. We were taking a much larger selection of hardware than before. The bivi tent was far too cumbersome; we decided to leave it behind and rely on finding good snow holes instead. Even without the tent, the snow stakes, ice screws, crampons and axes, rock gear, stoves, gas, food and sleeping bags all amounted to a daunting load.

Richard had decided to accompany us as far as the glacier, and we got away next morning at a steady pace under a hot sun. After an hour we reached the beginning of the glacier and started up a steep gully between the lower glacier moraines and a shield of ice-worn rock that formed the left bank of the glacier. Mud and rubble gave way to a jumble of boulders and scree. It was awkward scrambling round and over these obstacles, some of which were many times the size of a man, and it was all the more difficult with large sacks on our backs. Richard kept up well after two weeks at high altitude but a bristling series of ice spikes and mud-smeared glacier ice, visible from where we rested, presented a formidable obstacle to him in lightweight walking shoes. To get past, and up on to the glacier, we would have to negotiate a short, steep, ice cliff some 80 to 100 feet high. Large rocks were balanced precariously above the line of ascent.

'I don't think you should come any further,' Simon said. 'We could get you up there, but not back again.'

Richard looked around ruefully at the barren view of mud and perched boulders. He had been hoping for something more impressive than this. The West Face of Siula was not yet in view.

'I'll take your pictures before you go,' he announced. 'You never know, I might make a fortune selling them as obituary photos!'

'Much appreciated, I'm sure!' Simon muttered.

We left him there among the boulders. From our position high above on the ice cliffs he looked forlornly abandoned. He was in for a lonely time.

'Take care!' wafted up to us from cupped hands below.

'Don't worry,' Simon shouted, 'we don't intend sticking our necks out. We'll be back in time. See you . . .'

The lonely figure was soon lost amid the boulders as we headed up towards the first crevasses, where we put on our crampons and roped up. The heat of the glacier was intense under the glare reflected from icy mountain walls. There was not a breath of wind. The glacier edge was cracked and contorted, and we looked back at our route so as to fix the features in our minds. Neither of us wanted to forget it on the way down. Our tracks would certainly have disappeared under fresh snow by then, and it was important to know whether to go below or above the crevasses when we returned.

As a cold clear night came over the mountains we were cosily ensconced in our snow hole beneath the face. It would be a freezing early-morning start tomorrow.

2

TEMPTING FATE

It was cold. Five-in-the-morning cold, on a high Andean glacier. I struggled with zips and gaiters until my fingers would not work, and I rocked back and forward, hands in my crotch, moaning with the hot aches. It had never been this bad before, I thought, as the pain in my fingers fired up, but then I always thought that with hot aches. So damned painful.

Simon grinned at my agony. I knew that once warmed up I wouldn't get the aches again. It was some consolation.

'I'll go first, shall I?' Simon said, knowing he had me at a disadvantage. I nodded miserably, and he set off up the avalanche cone above our snow hole towards the icefield which reared up in blue early-morning ice.

Right then, this was it! I looked at Simon leaning above the small crevasse at the base of the face and planting his ice axe firmly into the steep ice wall above. The weather looked perfect. No tell-tale cloud front running a storm this time. If it held we'd be up and half-way down before the next bad spell.

I stamped my feet, trying to get my boots warmed up. Fragments of ice tinkled down on to my shoulders as Simon hammered axes up the ice, bunny-hopping his feet, then axes in again. I ducked from the cold shower, looking away to the south at the sky lightening by the minute above the summit of Sarapo.

When I next looked up Simon was nearly at the end of the rope, 150 feet above me. I had to crane my neck to see him. It was very steep.

29

Following his cheery shout I sorted out my axes, checked my crampons, and started up towards the wall. As I reached the crevasse I realised how precipitously steep it was. I felt off balance, forced out by the angle, until I had hauled myself out over the lip of the crevasse and up on to the ice wall. Stiff and unco-ordinated at first, I struggled unnecessarily until, warmed by the effort, my body began to flow into rhythmic movements, and a rush of exultation at being here set me off up towards the distant figure.

Simon stood on the outside of one foot, hanging back on the ice screws hammered into the ice, casual, relaxed:

'Steep, isn't it?'

'Almost vertical, that bit at the bottom,' I replied, 'but the ice is brilliant! I'll bet this is steeper than the Droites.'

Simon gave me the remaining screws and I carried on above him, sweating now, the morning cold driven off. Head down, keep looking at your feet, swing, swing, hop, look at your feet, swing swing ... all the way up a smooth 150 feet, no effort, no headache, feeling on top of the world. I drove in the screws, seeing the ice crack, split and protest – drive in, solid, clip in, lean back, relax. This was it!

I felt the flow, the heat and blood and strength flowing. It was right. 'Yeeee haaaaaaaa!' – listen to that echo, round and round the glacier. Thin wandering footprints, shadow lines, could be seen twisting up from the darker shadow of the collapsed snow hole on the glacier, already a long way down.

Simon was coming up, hitting hard, ice splintering down below him, hitting hard and strong, walking up on points of steel, head down, hitting, hopping, on past me and up, without a word, just hitting hard, breathing steady, getting smaller.

We climbed higher, 1,000 feet, 2,000, until we wondered when this icefield would end, and the rhythm became ragged with the monotony. We kept looking up and to our right, following the line we had chosen – a line that now looked different with the shortened perspective. The rock buttress swept up beside us into tangled gullies. Ribboned snow on the ledges, ice weeps and icicles everywhere, but where was the gully we wanted?

The sun was fully up; jackets and tops were in the sacks. Following Simon, I was slowing with the heat, dry-mouthed, wanting a drink. The angle eased. Looking to my right, I smiled seeing Simon with legs astride a large rock, sack off, taking a photograph of me as I came over the top edge of the icefield and headed towards him on an easy ramp line.

'Lunch,' he said, passing me a chocolate bar and some prunes. The gas stove hissed away busily, sheltered by his rucksack. 'The brew's nearly ready.'

I sat back, glad to rest in the sun and look around. It was past noon, and warm. Ice clattered down from the headwall which reared 2,000 feet above us. For the moment we were safe. The rock on which we lunched topped a slight rib, splitting the ground above the icefield so that the debris tumbled harmlessly past on either side. We sat, perched above the icefield, which was steeply sloped, dropping like a vertical wall beneath our lunch rock. A giddy, dragging sensation urged me to lean further out over the drop, pulling me down at the snow-ice sweeping away below. Looming over, with my stomach clenched, and a sharp strong sense of danger, I enjoyed the feeling.

Our footsteps and the snow hole were no longer visible, lost in the dazzling blur of white ice and white glacier. With the wind tonight all signs of our passing would be gone.

The upper tiers of the great yellow rock buttress which split the face crowded out our view of the way ahead. As we climbed up parallel with it, we began to see just how big it was – a respectable 1,000-foot-high wall which would have been a mountain in itself in the Dolomites. Stones had whirred down from the upper reaches all day, smacking into the right side of the icefield, then bouncing and wheeling down to the glacier. Thank God we hadn't climbed any nearer to the buttress! From a distance the stones seemed small and harmless, but the smallest, falling free from many hundreds of feet above, would have hurt us as surely as any rifle bullet.

We had to find the steep ice couloir which ran up through the side of this buttress, and would eventually lead us into the wide hanging gully we had seen from Seria Norte. This would be the key to the climb. We had under six hours to find it, climb it, and dig a comfortable snow cave in the gully above. A large ice cliff hung out from the edge of the hanging gully, streaming twenty- to thirty-foot icicles – free-hanging above the 200-foot wall below. That was what we wanted to get into, but it would be impossible to go directly up the wall through the fringe of icicles.

'How much higher do you reckon the couloir is?' I asked, seeing that Simon was examining the rocks intently.

'We'll have to go higher,' he said. 'It can't be that one.' He pointed to an extremely steep cascade of icicles just left of the ice cliff.

'It might go, but it isn't the one we saw. You're right, it's above that mixed ground.'

We wasted no more time. I put the stove away, and sorted out ice screws and axes before I led off, crossing the ramp, and then front-pointing up steepening water ice. The ice was harder and more brittle. I could see Simon, when I looked between my feet, ducking away from large chunks of ice that were breaking away from my axes. I heard his curses as some big pieces made painful direct hits.

Simon joined me at the belay and told me what he thought of my bombardment.

'Well, it's my turn now.'

He carried on up, following a slanting line to the right over bulges and areas of thin ice which showed the rock bared in places. I ducked away from some heavy ice fall, then more, before a warning doubt clicked in my head. Simon was above me, but off to the right! I looked up to see where the ice was coming from and saw the corniced summit ridge far above me. Some of the cornices overhung the West Face by as much as forty feet, and we were directly under their fall-line. Suddenly the day seemed less casual and relaxed. I watched Simon's progress, now agonisingly slow and hunched up, my hair bristling at the thought of a cornice collapse. I followed him as fast as I could. He too had realised the danger.

'Christ! Let's get out of here,' he said, passing me the ice screws.

I set off hurriedly. A cascade of ice dropped over steep underlying rocks in a fifty-foot step. I could see it was steep, 80° maybe, and hammered in a screw when I reached its base. I would climb it in one push, then move right.

Water was running under the ice, and in places the rock sparked as my axe hit it. I slowed down, climbing carefully, cautious of rushing into a mistake. Holding on to my left axe near the top of the cascade, I tiptoed out on my front points. Halfway into swinging my right axe, a sudden dark object rushed at me.

'Rocks!' I yelled, ducking down and away. Heavy blows thudded into my shoulder, whacking against my sack, and then it was past, and I watched Simon looking straight up at my warning. The boulder, about four-foot square, swept below me directly at him. It seemed an age before he reacted, and when he did it was with a slow-motion casualness which I found hard to believe. He leaned to his left and dropped his head as the heavy stone seemed to hit him full-on. I shut my eyes, and hunched harder as more stones hit me. When I looked again, Simon was all but hidden beneath the sack which he had swept up over his head.

'You okay?'

'Yes!' he shouted from behind his sack.

'I thought you were hit.'

'Only by small stuff. Get moving, I don't like it here.'

I climbed the last few feet of the cascade, and moved quickly right to the shelter of the rock. Simon grinned when he reached me:

'Where did that lot come from?'

'I don't know. I only saw it at the last moment. Too bloody close!'

'Let's get on. I can see the gully from here.'

Boosted with adrenalin, he climbed quickly towards the steep icy couloir visible in a corner of the main buttress. It was four-thirty. We had an hour and a half of light left.

I went on past his stance for another full rope length but the couloir seemed no nearer. The flat, white light made it hard to gauge distances. Simon set out on the last short pitch to the foot of the couloir.

'We ought to bivi here,' I said. 'It will be dark soon.'

'Yeah, but there's no chance of a snow hole, or any ledges.'

I could see he was right. Any night spent here would be uncomfortable. It was already getting hard to see.

'I'll try and get up this before dark.'

'Too late . . . it *is* dark!'

'Well, I bloody hope we can do it in one rope length then.' I didn't like the prospect of blundering around on steep ice in the dark trying to sort out belays.

I made a short traverse left to the foot of the couloir. 'Jesus! This is overhanging, and the ice is terrible!'

Simon said nothing.

Twenty feet of rotten honeycombed ice reared up in front of me, but above that I could see it relented and lay back to a more reasonable angle. I banged an ice screw into the good water ice at the foot of the wall, clipped the rope through it, turned my head-torch on, took a deep breath, and started climbing.

I was nervous at first for the angle forced me backwards, and the honeycombs crunched and sharded away beneath my feet, but the axes, biting deeper into harder ice, were solid and soon I was engrossed. A short panting struggle and the wall was beneath me, Simon no longer in sight. I stood on tiptoe on glassy hard water ice, blue in my torchlight, curving up above me into shadows.

The dark night silence was broken only by my axe blows and the wavering cone of light from my torch. The climbing held me completely, so that Simon might as well not have been there.

Hit hard. Hit again – that's it, now the hammer. Look at your feet. Can't see them. Kick hard, and again. On up, peering into shadows, trying to make out the line. The blue glass curves left, like a bob-sleigh run, the angle steepening under a huge fringe of icicles on the right. Is that another way up, behind the icicles? I move up, under the ice fringe. A few icicles break away, and thump tinkle down, chandelier sounds in the dark, and a muffled shout echoes up to me from below – no time to answer. This way is wrong. Damn, damn! Get back down, reverse it. No! Put a screw in.

I fumble at my harness for a screw but can't find one – forget it, just get back below the icicles.

I shouted down to Simon when I reached the couloir again, but I couldn't hear his reply. Spindrift powder rushed down in a burst from above. Unexpected, it made my heart leap.

I had no ice screws. I had forgotten to take them from Simon and had used my only screw down at the bottom. I did not know what to do, 120 feet up very steep ice. Go back down? I was scared of the unprotected drop beneath me, and of the idea of needing an ice screw for a belay if I couldn't find any rock. I shouted again but there was no reply. Take a few breaths and get on with it!

I could see the top of the couloir fifteen feet above me, the last ten feet rearing up steeply, tube-shaped, the good ice giving way to mushy powder. I bridged across the tube, legs splayed against yielding snow. I flailed my axes, dreading the 240-foot fall below me on to one ice screw, and thrashed about me, breathing quick, frightened gasps of effort before I could pull myself out on to the easy snow slopes above the couloir.

When I had regained my breath, I climbed up to a rock wall and arranged a belay in the loose cracks and blocks.

Simon joined me, breathing hard. 'You took your time,' he snapped.

I bristled. 'It was bloody hard, and I was as good as solo-ing it. I had no screws with me.'

'Forget it. Let's find a bivi.'

It was ten o'clock, and the wind had got up, making the minus-fifteen temperature seem a lot colder. Tired and irritable after a hard fifteen-hour day, we had dreaded the hour or so it would take us to dig a snow hole.

'Nothing doing here,' I said, eyeing the slope critically. 'Not deep enough to dig.'

'I could try that dollop up there.'

Simon indicated a huge golf-ball of snow, fifty feet across, which clung defiantly to the vertical rock wall thirty feet above us. He moved up to it and cautiously started prodding it with his axe. On my shaky belay, I appreciated his caution, for I would be swept away if it suddenly parted company with the wall.

'Joe!' Simon yelled. 'Wow! You're not going to believe this.' I heard a piton being hammered into rock, and a few more squeaks of joy, and then the call to come up to him.

I felt dubious, and gingerly poked my head through the small hole Simon had made.

'Good God!'

'I said you wouldn't believe it.' Simon sat back comfortably on his sack, belayed to a good strong peg, and waved regally at his new domain. 'And it has a bathroom,' he said with glee, all tiredness and bad humour gone.

The snow was hollow. Inside there was one large chamber, almost high enough to stand in, and beside it another smaller cave. Here was a ready-made palace!

Yet, as we got organised and settled into our sleeping bags, I could not help turning over in my head my usual dislike of bivi sites, trying to assess the safety margin. I had good reason to be alarmed about the precarious state of this one, and Simon knew why, but there was no point in harping on about it. There was nowhere else.

There had been no alternative, as I remembered all too vividly, two years earlier when climbing on the Bonatti Pillar on the south-west side of Les Petits Drus. I was elated to have made such fast progress with Ian Whittaker up the 2,000-foot golden-red granite spire which dominates the view from the Chamonix valley. The architectural magnificence of its lines drawn sharply by the shadows of the sun against the softer backdrop of the whole range of the French Alps had made this climb one of the most aesthetically pleasing routes in the Alps. We had climbed well that day to establish ourselves by nightfall just a few hundred feet from the summit, though still on very steep and difficult ground. There was no possibility of reaching the top that night, nor was there need for haste in seeking a ledge on which to sleep, for the weather was clear and settled, and we would certainly reach the top the following day. It would be another warm night, and this high up, at 12,000 feet, the sky would be brilliant with stars.

Ian had climbed above my small stance overlooking the airy sweep of the precipitous walls below. The corner he was following was relentlessly steep and failing light made him painfully slow. I waited, shivering in the chill evening air, hopping from foot to foot, trying to regain circulation despite my cramped position. I was tired after the long day and yearned to lie back and rest in comfort.

At last a muffled shout told me he had found something, and soon I was cursing and struggling in the gathering dusk up the corner Ian had just led. Even before it had darkened I had spotted that we were slightly off route. We had climbed directly up a steep crack splitting a vertical wall instead of traversing to the right. This had placed us beneath a huge overhang about 150 feet above us. No doubt we would have to resort to complicated diagonal abseiling in the morning to get past it. For now, it had its advantages: at least we would be protected from any rockfall during the night.

I found Ian sitting on a ledge about four feet wide but long enough for the two of us to lie down foot-to-head. It would be quite adequate for a night's sleep. As I climbed up to him I noticed in my torchlight that the ledge was in fact the top of a large pedestal fixed to the vertical wall above the corner we had just climbed. It was solid and gave us no reason to think it might be unsafe.

An hour later we had fixed a handrail safety rope, strung between an old ring peg and a spike of rock, clipped ourselves in and settled down to sleep.

The next few seconds were unforgettable.

I was inside a protective waterproof bivouac bag, half-asleep, and Ian was making final adjustments to his safety line. Suddenly and without warning, I felt myself drop swiftly. Simultaneously there was an ear-splitting roar and grinding. With my head inside the bag and my arms flailing outside the opening at my chest I knew nothing except the sickening dread as I went plummeting down into the 2,000-foot abyss below. I heard a high-pitched yelp of fear amid the heavy roaring, then felt a springy recoil. The safety rope had held. All my weight was held on my armpits, as I had accidentally caught the safety rope in the fall. I swung gently on the rope, trying to remember whether I had tied-in to the rope and gripping my arms tight just in case.

The thunderous sound of tons of granite plunging down the pillar echoed and then died to silence.

I was completely disorientated. The silence seemed frighteningly ominous. Where was Ian? I thought of that fleeting yelp, and was horrified by the idea that perhaps he had not tied-on after all.

'By 'eck!' I heard close by in gruff Lancastrian.

I struggled to get my head out of the tightly squeezed bag. Ian was hanging beside me on the V-shaped safety rope. His head was lolling on his chest, his head-torch casting a yellow glow on to the surrounding rock. I could see blood on his neck.

I fumbled inside my bag for my head-torch, and then, carefully lifting the elastic torch strap from his blood-matted hair, I examined his injury. He had trouble talking at first, for he had hit his head hard in the fall. Fortunately the cut was a minor one, but the shock of the fall, while half-asleep in the dark, had completely confused us. It took some time to realise that the whole pedestal had detached itself from the pillar and dropped straight off the mountain face. There was a good deal of nervous swearing and hysterical giggling as, gradually, we became aware of the seriousness of our position.

At last, we fell silent. A terrible fear and insecurity had overtaken our boisterous reaction to the unimaginable event. Shining torches below, we saw the remains of our two ropes, which had been hanging beneath the ledge. They were cut to pieces, shredded by the falling rock. Turning round to inspect the safety line, we were appalled to find that the old ring peg on which we hung was moving, and that the spike of rock had been badly damaged. It looked as if one of the two attachment points would give way at any moment. We knew that if just one anchor point failed we would both be hurled into the void. We quickly searched for our equipment to see how we might improve the anchors, only to find that all of it, including our boots, had fallen with the ledge. So confident had we been in the safety of the ledge that we hadn't thought it necessary to clip our gear to the rope. We could do nothing.

To attempt to climb up or down would have been suicidal. The shadow of the huge overhang above us put paid to any idea of climbing in socks without ropes. Beneath stood a vertical wall hidden by the darkness – an obstacle we could descend only on ropes. The nearest ledges were 200 feet below, and we would certainly fall to our deaths long before we got anywhere near them.

We hung on that fragile rope for twelve interminable hours. Eventually our shouts were heard and a rescue helicopter succeeded in plucking us from the wall. The experience of that long, long night, expecting to fall at any time, one minute laughing hysterically, then silence, always with stomachs clenched, petrified, waiting for something we did not wish to think about, will never be forgotten.

Ian returned to the Alps the following summer, but his desire to climb had been destroyed. He returned home vowing never to go to the Alps again. I was lucky, or stupid, and got over my dread – except when it came to bivouacs.

'What shall it be then?' Simon held up two foil bags. 'Moussaka or Turkey Supreme?'

'Who gives a toss! They're both disgusting!'

'Good choice. We'll have the Turkey.'

Two brews of passion fruit and a few prunes later we settled back for sleep.

3

STORM AT·THE SUMMIT

Getting organised in the morning was a much easier business than it had been previously. We had the advantage of standing room when it came to rolling up Karrimats, packing sleeping bags, and sorting out the climbing gear that had been dropped in a tangled mess on our arrival the night before.

It was my turn to lead. Simon remained inside the snow cave, belayed to a rock piton, while I gingerly stepped out of the small entrance on to the sloped ice of the gully we had ascended in the dark. The ground was unfamiliar to me. I was standing on good ice which funnelled down into a narrowing curved cone below me before disappearing into the top of the tube which I had struggled so hard to get out of last night. The huge icefield we had climbed yesterday was no longer visible. I looked over to my right. A short distance above me the top of the gully reared up in a vertical cascade of ice, but over on its far side I could see that the angle eased and there was a way up and past the cascade into another gully above.

I tiptoed to the right, stopping to drive in a screw before launching up the side of the cascade. It was excellent water ice and I enjoyed the aggressive warming work. I glanced back at the entrance of the snow cave and saw Simon peeping out, feeding the rope as I climbed. The structure of the natural cave looked even more impressive than it had last night and I couldn't help wondering at our good fortune to have found it, for a night spent in the open at the top of the gully would have been, to say the least, uncomfortable.

Above the cascade I ran out the rest of the rope, following a snowy gully. Simon quickly joined me.

'Just as we thought,' I said. 'We should reach the hanging ramp on the next pitch.'

He set off to the right before disappearing from the minor gully, where I stood resting, into the key ramp line we had seen so long ago on Seria Norte. I reckoned that the main difficulties were now behind us and it would be only a matter of running it out to the top of the ramp, and then up the summit slopes.

When I joined Simon in the ramp I realised that our problems were not over. At the top of the ramp we could see that there was a formidable barrier of tooth-shaped seracs with no apparent way through them. The vertical rock walls on each side of the ramp would be impossibly hard to ascend, and the seracs stretched from wall to wall without a break.

'Damn!'

'Yeah, it's bad news. I wasn't expecting those.'

'There may be an exit,' I said. 'If not, we're stuck.'

'Bloody hope not! It's a long way back.'

I looked at the near-by peaks, trying to gauge our height on the mountain.

'We bivied at five eight hundred metres last night. That's what? Nineteen thousand feet . . . right, that means we have about fifteen hundred to go,' I said.

'Two thousand, more like.'

'Okay, two, but we did at least two and a half thousand on harder ground yesterday so we should top out today.'

'I wouldn't be so sure. Depends on how hard that exit is, and remember the last bit is all flutings.'

I set off up the 55° ramp and made fast progress. We alternated leads, rarely talking to each other, concentrating on forcing the pace. Yesterday we had used ice screws to protect each rope length, and the steep ice had slowed us down. Today we could feel the thin air taking its toll where the easier ground enabled us to climb an almost continuous double pitch, kicking steps up to the leader for 150 feet, and then up past him for the same again.

41

I was breathing heavily as I dug through the soft surface snow to find the firm ice below. I drove in two ice screws and planted both axes above my stance before tying into them and shouting for Simon to come up. We were close to the serac barrier, having climbed 1,000 feet up the ramp. I checked my watch: one o'clock. We had overslept and made a late start, but, after ten pitches in four and a half hours, we had made up for it. I felt confident and at ease. We were a match for this route and I now knew that we would finish it. I felt a thrill at the knowledge that I was, at last, on the verge of achieving a first ascent, and a hard one at that.

As Simon panted up, the sun crept over the seracs at the top of the ramp and spilled bright white light down the sweep of snow below us. Simon was grinning broadly. I needed no explanation for his good humour. It was one of those moments when everything came together, and there were no struggles or doubts, and nothing more to do but enjoy the sensation.

'May as well get past the seracs and then rest.'

'Sure,' Simon agreed, as he studied the barrier above. 'See those icicles? That's the way past.'

I looked at the cascade of ice and, at first, I dismissed it as too difficult. It was clearly overhanging at the bottom. A leaning wall of smooth blue ice with a huge fringe of icicles dripping from its head provided the only solid surface across the otherwise powdery seracs. Yet, this cascade was the only weakness that I could spot in the barrier. If we were to attempt it, we would have to climb the initial ice wall for some twenty-five feet and then break a way through the icicles and continue up the more reasonably angled cascade ice above.

'It looks hard.'

'Yes. I'd prefer to attempt the rock first.'

'It's loose as hell.'

'I know, but it might go. I'll give it a try anyway.'

He moved some pitons, a few wires, and a couple of 'Friends' round to the front of his harness before edging left to the start of the rock wall. I was anchored firmly, just below and to the right of the cascade. The rock, yellow and crumbly, bordered the vertical powdery snow between the cascade and the rocky side of the ramp.

I watched Simon carefully, for I knew that if he fell it would be with the sudden violence of hand- or foot-holds breaking away and not the gradual surrender to waning strength. He placed the camming device in a crack as high up the wall as he could. It expanded evenly into the crack with each of its four cams pressed hard against the rock. I guessed that it would be the rock which would break away, and not the 'Friend', if Simon fell.

He stepped up cautiously, testing his foot-holds with light kicks, and hitting the holds above his head to check their looseness. He hesitated a moment, stretched against the wall, gripping the rock above him at full reach, and then began to pull himself up slowly. I tensed, holding the ropes locked in the sticht plate, so that I could hold his fall immediately.

Suddenly, the holds tore loose from the wall, and for a second Simon held his poise, his hands still outstretched but now gripping two lumps of loose rock. Then he was off, falling backwards into the gully below. I braced myself, expecting the 'Friend' to rip out as well, but it held firm, and I stopped his short tumble with ease.

'Brilliant!' I said, laughing at the surprise on his face.

'Shit! . . . I was sure those were solid.'

When he had got back to me he looked at the cascade again.

'I don't fancy doing it directly, but if I can get past the right side I should be able to crack it.'

'The ice looks mushy there.'

'We'll see.'

He launched himself up the right side of the cascade, avoiding the steep wall but attempting to make a slight traverse to the right before climbing back left above the icicles. Unfortunately the ice gave way to honeycombed snow and sugary ice crystals. He managed to reach a point parallel with the top of the icicles before the conditions became impossible and he could go no higher. He was twenty feet above me, and for a while it seemed as if he was stuck: reversing what he had just climbed would be to invite a nasty fall. Eventually he succeeded in fixing a sling around a thick icicle which had rejoined the cascade to form a loop, and he abseiled off this down to my stance.

'I'm knackered. You have a go.'

'Okay, but I'd move further to the side if I were you. I'll have to knock most of those icicles away.'

Many of them were as thick as a man's arm and nearly five feet long. Some even bigger. I started up the ice wall, which pushed me back off balance, and at once I felt the strain on my arms. The sack on my back pulled me away from the ice. I bunny-hopped my crampons quickly up the wall, smashing my axes hard into the brittle ice above, pulling up, hopping again – all the time trying to save my strength by climbing fast. As I neared the icicles I realised that I would be unable to hold on for very much longer; already I was too tired to break away the icicles while holding on to the wall with one axe. I swung as hard as I could until my axe bit in deeply, and was firm enough to hold me. I then clipped my harness into the wrist-loop on the axe and hung wearily from it. I kept a wary eye on the axe tip embedded in the ice, and only when I was sure it was holding my full weight safely did I extract my hammer axe from the wall and, reaching above me, hammer an ice screw into the wall.

I clipped the rope through the screw and breathed a sigh of relief. At least there was no longer a danger of falling more than five or six feet. The icicles were within easy reach. Without thinking I swung my hammer through the fringe of ice and, even more stupidly, looked up at what I was doing. The best part of a hundredweight of icicles smashed down on to my head and shoulders and clattered away down on to Simon. We both started swearing. I cursed myself and the sharp pain of a split lip and cracked tooth, and Simon cursed me.

'Sorry . . . didn't think.'

'Yeah. I noticed.'

When I looked up again I saw that although it was painful the hammer had done the trick and there was now a way clear through to the easier-angled ice above. It didn't take long to swarm up the top of the wall and run the remainder of the rope to a belay in the wide shallow gully above.

Simon came up covered in ice particles and frosted white by the powder snow which had swept down the cascade. He carried on past me to a slight ridge which marked the end of the ramp and the start of the summit slopes. He had lit the gas stove and cleared a place to sit in comfort by the time I joined him.

'Your mouth is bleeding,' he said flatly.

'It's nothing. It was my fault anyway.'

It was noticeably colder now that we were away from the shelter of the ice gullies and exposed to a steady breeze. For the first time we could see the summit, formed from a huge overhanging cornice which bulged out over the slopes 800 feet above us. The ridge sweeping off to the left would be our line of descent, but we couldn't see it very well in the swirling clouds which were steadily spilling over from the east. It looked as if bad weather was on the way.

Simon passed me a hot drink and then huddled deeper into his jacket with his back to the bitter wind. He was looking at the summit slopes, searching for the best line of ascent. It was the state of the snow on this last part of the route that worried us more than the angle or the technical difficulties. The whole slope was corrugated by powder flutings which had gradually built up as fresh snow had sloughed down the face. We had heard all about Peruvian flutings and hadn't liked the stories; it was best not to attempt them. The weather patterns in Europe never produced such horrors. South American mountains were renowned for these spectacular snow and ice creations, where powder snow seemed to defy gravity and form 70°, even 80° slopes, and ridges developed into tortured unstable cornices of huge size, built up one on top of the other. On any other mountains the powder would have swept on down and only formed on much easier-angled slopes.

Above us a rock band cut across the whole slope. It was not steep, but was powdered with a treacherous coating of snow. After 100 feet it merged back into the snow slope, which grew steeper as it climbed up. The flutings started shortly above the rock band and continued without break to the summit. Once we had established ourselves in the gully formed between two flutings we would have to force a way to the top, for it would be impossible to traverse out by crossing a fluting and getting into the neighbouring gully. It would be vitally important to choose the right gully, and we could see that many of them closed down into dead-ends as two flutings merged together. If I looked carefully I could make out a few gullies which did not close down, but as soon as I tried to look at the whole slope these became lost in the maze of gullies and flutings streaming down the face.

'Christ! It looks desperate!' Simon said. 'I can't work out a way up at all.'

'I can't see us getting to the top today.'

'Not if those clouds unload, that's for sure. What time is it?'

'Four o'clock. Two hours' light left. Better get moving.'

I wasted valuable time trying to cross the rock band. It was tilted like a steep roof, but unlike the rock in the ramp it was black and compact with only a few small holds mostly hidden beneath the snow. I knew it wasn't difficult, but I was standing on an open face with a drop of nearly 4,000 feet below me and felt very unnerved by the exposure. There was also a long gap of unprotected rope between me and Simon who was belaying me from our resting place. His only anchor was his axes buried in the snow, and I knew all too well how useless these would be if I made a mistake.

My left foot slipped and the crampon points skittered on the rock. I hated this sort of delicate balance climbing, but I was committed to it now; no going back. As I balanced on two small edges of rock, front points teetering on the verge of slipping, my legs began to tremble and I shouted a warning to Simon. I could hear the fear in my voice and cursed myself for letting Simon know it. I tried moving up again, but my nerve failed me and I couldn't complete the move. I knew it would take just a couple of moves to reach easier ground, and tried convincing myself that if this wasn't so terrifyingly exposed I would walk up it, hands in pockets, but I couldn't shake off the fear. I was gripped.

The West Face of Siula Grande in the Peruvian Andes. (Photo: Gary Kinsey)

Above: Joe (left) and Richard walking in to base camp. (Photo: Simon Yates)

Left: Norma and Gloria visit the camp. (Photo: Joe Simpson)

Quebrada Sampococha where the girls tended their cattle. (Photo: Yates)

Relaxing at base camp before the climb. (Photo: Simpson)

Joe crossing the moraines on an early reconnaissance. (Photo: Yates)

Setting out for the climb – Simon by the coppered green lake on the approach to the West Face. (Photo: Simpson)

Yerupaja looms above Joe as he approaches the glacier. (Photo: Yates)

Difficult route-finding through the crevasses at the foot of the glacier.
(Photo: Simpson)

Joe climbing the icefield on the first day. (Photo: Yates)

Joe exiting the icefield and heading for the ramp above the V-shaped crux couloir to the right of his rucksack (*above*). Joe on the cascades (*below*) seconds before the rockfall. (Photos: Yates)

Joe climbs the last of the flutings, the glacier 4,500 feet below. (Photo: Yates)

The route up, and the route down, the treacherous ice cliff visible on the left. See map on p. 49. (Photo: Simpson)

Gradually, I calmed down and carefully thought out the few moves I needed to make. When I tried again I was surprised at how easy it seemed. I was above the difficulty and climbing quickly up easy ground before I realised it. The belay was little better than Simon's and I warned him of this before he started after me. The sudden fright still had me breathing hard and it annoyed me to see Simon climb easily over the difficulties and know that I had lost control and let fear get the better of me.

'God! I was gripped stupid on that,' I said.

'I noticed.'

'Which gully should we go for?' I had looked for a likely one but found it impossible to see, when close up to them, whether they closed off or not.

'I don't know. That one is the widest. I'll have a look at that.'

Simon entered the gully and immediately began floundering in deep powder. The sides of the flutings rose up fifteen feet on either side of him. There was no chance of changing line. Spindrift avalanches poured down on to his struggling figure so that sometimes he disappeared from sight. The light was going rapidly, and I noticed that it had begun to snow, the spindrift getting heavier. I was directly beneath Simon and, after sitting still for two hours, I was chilled to the bone. Simon was excavating huge quantities of snow down on to me and I could do nothing to avoid it.

I switched my head-torch on and was surprised to see that it was eight o'clock. Four hours to climb 300 feet. I seriously doubted whether we would be able to get up these flutings. At last, a distant, muffled shout from the snow-filled clouds told me to follow on. I was dangerously cold, despite having put on my polar jacket and windproof. We would have to bivouac somewhere on these horrendous slopes because sitting still for such a long time while belaying was out of the question. I couldn't believe what Simon had done to climb that rope length up the gully. He had dug a trench four feet deep by four wide all the way up it; his exhausting search for more solid snow yielding a weak layer of crusted ice which barely held his weight. Most of this had been broken away as he had climbed, so that I had great difficulty following his lead. It had taken him three hours to climb, and when I reached him I could see that it had tired him out. I felt very tired, too, and cold, and it was important we bivouacked soon.

'I can't believe this snow!'

'Bloody terrifying. I thought I was falling off all the way up.'

'We have to bivi. I was freezing down there.'

'Yeah, but not here. The fluting has got too small.'

'Okay. You may as well lead up again.'

I knew it would be easier and avoid rope tangles, but I regretted not being able to keep moving. Two freezing and interminable hours later I joined Simon 100 feet higher up. He was belayed in a large hole he had dug into the base of the gully.

'I've found some ice.'

'Good enough for an ice screw?'

'Well it's better than nothing. If you get in here we can enlarge this sideways.'

I squeezed in beside him, fully expecting the floor of the cave to collapse down the gully at any moment. We began digging into the sides of the flutings, slowly enlarging the cave into a long rectangular snow hole set across the gully, with the entrance partially filled up by our excavations.

By eleven o'clock we had settled into our sleeping bags, eaten the last freeze-dried meal, and were savouring a last hot drink of the day.

'Three hundred feet to go. I just hope it isn't worse than what we've just done.'

'At least the storm has stopped. But it's damned cold. I think my little finger is frostbitten. It's white down to the hand.'

It must have been close to minus twenty when we had been exposed to the spindrift in the gullies, and the wind had brought the wind chill temperature down nearer to minus forty. We were lucky to have found a place for a snow-hole.

I hoped we would have clear sunny weather tomorrow.

The base of the gas canister was coated in a thick layer of ice. I knocked it against my helmet and managed to remove most of it, then I stuffed it deep into my sleeping bag, feeling the icy metal against my thighs. Five minutes later I was snuggled in again with only my nose sticking out of the bag, and one eye keeping a sleepy watch on the stove. It roared busily, but it was dangerously close to my bag. Blue light shone through the cave walls. It had been a long and bitterly cold night at 20,000 feet, perhaps nearer 21,000.

When the water was boiling I sat up and hurriedly donned my polar jacket, windproof and gloves. I fumbled in the snow wall of the cave looking for the sachet of fruit juice and the chocolate.

'Brew's ready.'

'God's teeth! I'm bloody freezing.'

Simon uncurled from his cramped foetal position, took the

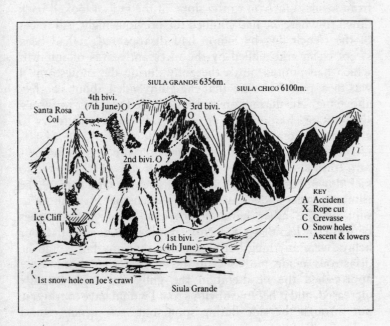

steaming mug and disappeared back into his bag. I drank slowly, hugging the hot cup to my chest, watching the second lot of snow melt down in the pan. The gas flame was not so strong.

'How much gas have we got left?' I asked.

'One tin. Is that one empty?'

'Not quite. We may as well drink as much as it will produce and save the other for the descent.'

'Yeah. We haven't got much fruit juice left either. Just one packet.'

'We'll have judged it right, then. Enough for one more bivi, that's all we need.'

It was a long, cold business gearing up, but that was the least of my worries. The flutings lay ahead and it was my turn to lead. To make things more difficult I had to exit the cave and somehow climb over the roof, which stretched the full width of the gully. I succeeded, but not without destroying most of the cave and burying Simon, who had belayed me from inside. Once on to the slope of the gully I looked back down to where we had climbed the previous night. All traces of the trench dug by Simon had disappeared. It had been swept clean and refilled by the incessant waves of spindrift which had poured down the gully during the snowstorm. I was disappointed to see that the gully ended about 100 feet above me. The flutings on each side joined together to form a single razor-sharp ribbon of powder. I would have to try to cross over into another fluting after all.

The sky was clear and there was no wind. It was Simon's turn to sit stoically under the deluge of snow I was forced to kick down, but daylight had dubious advantages. It made the climbing easier and allowed me to see whether I was about to slip; on the other hand it provided unnerving glimpses between my legs of 4,500 feet of emptiness. Knowing that our belays were anything but secure and that any fall would be disastrous made me concentrate on the way ahead. As I approached the dead-end in the gully the angle steadily increased, and it became obvious that I would have to traverse out through the side fluting soon; but . . . which one? I couldn't see over the sides of the flutings and had no idea what I would be traversing into. I looked down and saw Simon watching me intently. Only his head and chest stuck out from the roof of the cave, and the huge drop framed behind him emphasised the precariousness of our position. I could see that the flutings were not as high near the cave, and that Simon might be able to see more of the way ahead than I could.

'Which way should I go? Can you see anything?'

'Don't go left.'

'Why?'

'It seems to drop away, and it looks bloody dangerous!'

'What's on the right?'

'Can't see, but the flutings are not so steep. It's a lot better than the left anyway.'

I hesitated. Once I started ploughing through a fluting I might be unable to return. I didn't want to find myself in an even worse position. However high I stretched I couldn't see into the gully on my right. I wasn't even sure there would be a gully there, and none of the snow I could see above me gave any idea of what might be awaiting me.

'Okay. Watch the ropes,' I shouted as I began to dig into the right-hand side of the gully. Then I laughed at what I had just said. It would do no good concentrating on belaying if the belay was going to rip straight out.

To my surprise, digging furiously with both axes into the fluting was no harder than climbing the gully, and I emerged, breathing hard, on the other side, in an identical steepening gully above which I could see the huge cornice of the summit only a rope's length away. Simon floundered up to me and whooped when he saw the summit behind me.

'Cracked it,' he said.

'I hope so, but this last bit looks bloody steep.'

'It'll go.' He set off up the slope churning huge amounts of freezing snow down on to my exposed belay hole. I pulled my hood over my helmet and turned my back, gazing down at the glacier far below me. Suddenly our exposed stance appalled me. The loose snow was so steep and my belay so precarious that I felt a sickening disbelief in what we were doing. An excited yell tore me from my thoughts and I turned to see the rope disappearing over the top of the gully above.

'Done it. No more flutings. Come up.'

He was sitting, legs astride a fluting, grinning manically, when I pulled myself wearily out of the gully. Behind him, less than fifty feet from us, the summit cornice reared up in a threatening bulge of snow-ice which overhung the West Face. I quickly moved past Simon and cramponed on firm snow up and to the left, where the summit cornice was smallest. Ten minutes later, I stood beneath the snow ridge dividing West Face from East.

'Take a photo.'

I waited until Simon had his camera ready before planting my axe over the ridge on to the east side and heaving myself over onto the broad-backed col under the summit. For the first time in four days I had a new view on which to feast. The sun bathed the snow sweeping down into the eastern glacier. After the long, cold, shadowed days on the West Face it felt luxurious to sit there warmed by the sun. I had forgotten that, now we were climbing in the Southern Hemisphere, everything was the wrong way round: South Faces here were the equivalent of icy cold North Faces in the Alps, and East Faces became West. No wonder the mornings had been so cold and shadowed and we had to wait until late in the day before being blessed with a few hours' sunshine.

Simon joined me and we laughed happily as we took off our sacks and sat on them, carelessly dropping axes and mitts in the snow, content to be quiet a while and look around us.

'Let's leave the sacks here and go up to the summit,' Simon said, interrupting my self-indulgent reverie. The summit! Of course, I had forgotten we had only reached the ridge. Escaping from the West Face had seemed to be an end in itself. I looked up at the icecream cone rising behind Simon. It was only about 100 feet away.

'You go ahead. I'll take some photos when you reach the top'.

He grabbed some chocolate and sweets before getting up

and tramping slowly up through soft snow. The altitude was having its effect. When he was outlined against the sky, bending over his axe on top of the spectacular summit cornice, I began feverishly snapping photographs. Leaving the sacks at the col, I followed, breathing hard, and feeling the tiredness in my legs.

We took the customary summit photos and ate some chocolate. I felt the usual anticlimax. What now? It was a vicious circle. If you succeed with one dream, you come back to square one and it's not long before you're conjuring up another, slightly harder, a bit more ambitious – a bit more dangerous. I didn't like the thought of where it might be leading me. As if, in some strange way, the very nature of the game was controlling me, taking me towards a logical but frightening conclusion; it always unsettled me, this moment of reaching the summit, this sudden stillness and quiet after the storm, which gave me time to wonder at what I was doing and sense a niggling doubt that perhaps I was inexorably losing control – was I here purely for pleasure or was it egotism? Did I really want to come back for more? But these moments were also good times, and I knew that the feelings would pass. Then I could excuse them as morbid pessimistic fears that had no sound basis.

'Looks like we are in for another storm,' Simon said.

He had been quietly examining the North Ridge, our line of descent, which was rapidly being obscured by massed clouds rolling up the East Face and tumbling out over on to the west side. Even now I could see little of the ridge, and the glacier up which we had made our approach would be completely covered within the hour. The ridge began where we had left our sacks and rose to a subsidiary summit before twisting back on itself and curling down into the clouds. I saw snatches of frighteningly steep razor-edges through cloud gaps, and some dangerously corniced sections, the East Face dropping away to the right in a continuous flank of tortured flutings. We would be unable to traverse below the corniced ridge at a safe distance. The flutings looked impassable.

'Jesus! It looks hairy.'

'Yeah. Better get our skates on. If we move quickly we can traverse under that summit and then rejoin the ridge further down. In fact, I don't think we'll even have an hour.'

Simon held out his hand, and the first snowflakes drifted down lazily on to his glove.

We returned to the sacks and then set off to circle around the minor summit. Simon led the way. We moved roped together, with coils of rope in hand in case of a fall. It was the fastest way and, with the deep powder snow hampering our progress, it was our only chance of getting past the minor summit in reasonable visibility. If Simon fell I hoped to have time enough to get my axe buried; though I doubted whether the axe would find any purchase in the loose snow.

The clouds closed in on us after half an hour, when we were on the east flank of the second summit. Ten minutes later we were lost in the white-out. There was no wind, and the snow fell silently in large heavy flakes. It was about two-thirty and we knew it would snow until late evening. We stood in silence, staring around us, trying to make out where we were.

'I think we should head down.'

'I don't know . . . no, not down. We must keep in touch with the ridge. Didn't you see those flutings on this side. We'd never get back up again.'

'Have we got past that second summit?'

'I think so, yes.'

'I can't see anything up there.'

The snow and cloud merged into a uniform blank whiteness. I could see no difference between snow and sky further than five feet from me.

'Wish we had a compass.'

As I spoke I noticed a lightening in the cloud above us. The sun, shining weakly through the murk, cast the faintest of shadows on the ridge 100 feet above us, but before I had a chance to tell Simon, it was gone.

'I've just seen the ridge.'

'Where?'

'Straight above us. Can't see a thing now, but I definitely saw it.'

'Right, I'll climb up and find it. If you stay here you'll have better luck stopping me if I don't see the edge of the ridge in time.'

He set off, and after a short time I had only the ropes moving through my hands to show me he was there. The snow fall was getting heavier. I felt the first twinges of anxiety. This ridge had turned out to be a lot more serious than we had ever imagined while our attention had been focused on the route up the West Face. I was about to call out to Simon and ask if he could see anything, but the words died on my lips as the ropes suddenly whipped out through my gloves. At the same time a deep, heavy explosion of sound echoed through the clouds. The ropes ran unchecked through my wet icy gloves for a few feet then tugged sharply at my harness, pulling me chest-first into the snow slope. The roaring died away.

I knew at once what had happened. Simon must have fallen through the corniced ridge, yet the volume of sound suggested something more like a serac avalanche. I waited. The ropes remained taut with his body weight.

'Simon!' I yelled. 'You okay?'

There was no answer. I decided to wait before attempting to move up towards the ridge. If he was hanging over the west side I reckoned it would be some time before he sorted himself out and managed to regain the ridge. After about fifteen minutes I heard Simon shouting unintelligibly. The weight had come off the rope, and I climbed towards him until I could make out what he was saying.

'I've found the ridge!'

I had gathered *that*, and laughed nervously. He had indeed found a lot more of the ridge than he had bargained for. I stopped grinning when I reached him. He was standing shakily just below the crest.

'I thought I'd had it there,' he muttered, suddenly sitting down heavily in the snow as if his legs had failed him. 'Bloody hell . . . that was it! The whole bloody thing fell off. God!'

He shook his head as if trying to dislodge what he had just seen. When the fright eased, and his body stopped pumping adrenalin, he looked back at the edge of the ridge, and quietly told me what had happened:

'I never saw the ridge. I just glimpsed an edge of it far away to the left. There was no warning. No crack. One minute I was climbing, the next I was falling. It must have broken away forty feet back from the edge. It broke behind me, I think; or under my feet. Either way it took me down instantly. It was so *fast*! I had no time to think. I didn't know what the hell was going on, except that I was falling.'

'I'll bet!' I looked at the drop of the face behind him as he bowed his head and breathed hard, one hand on his thigh trying to stop the tell-tale tremor in his leg.

'I was tumbling all over the place and everything seemed to be happening in slow motion. I forgot I was tied to the rope. The noise and the falling – it just stopped me understanding anything. I can remember seeing all these huge blocks of snow falling with me, they fell at the same speed at first, and I thought "this is it". They were massive. Ten- . . . twenty-foot-square chunks.'

He was calmer now, but I shivered at the thought of what would have happened if I had moved up with him – it would have taken both of us.

'Then I felt the rope at my waist, but I thought it would just come down with me. I wasn't stopping, and all the blocks were smashing against me, flipping me over.'

He paused again, then continued: 'It was much lighter below me, and the blocks tumbled away from me down an enormous drop of space, spinning and breaking up. I kept getting glimpses of this as the snow walloped into me and spun me round . . . Perhaps I wasn't falling by then, but all the thumping and spinning made it feel as if I was. It seemed to be going on and on and on . . . I wasn't scared then, just totally confused and numb. As if real time was standing still and there was no longer time to be frightened.'

When he did finally stop, he was hanging in space, and could see over to his left the ridge still peeling away. The cloud on the east side blocked the view slightly, but great blocks of snow were falling from the cloud and went crashing down the face below, as if the ridge was breaking away from him.

'At first I was so disoriented I wasn't sure whether I was safe or not. I had to think it out before I realised that you had held my fall. The drop below me was horrific. I could see right down the West Face, 4,500 feet, clear all the way to the glacier. I was in a panic for a while. The huge drop had appeared so suddenly beneath me, and I was hanging thirty feet below the ridge line, not touching the slope. The headwall of the West Face was directly beneath me. I could see our route up the icefield!'

'If that cornice had come down we would just have disappeared without trace,' I ventured. 'How did you get back?'

'Well, I tried to get back on to the ridge, and it turned out to be one hell of a struggle. The break-line left by the cornice was vertical snow and nearly thirty feet high. I didn't know if what was left after the collapse was safe. When I finally got up I heard you shouting from down on the East Face and I was nearly too tired to answer. I still couldn't see an end to the fresh break-line on the ridge. It seemed close to 200 feet. Funny how the visibility cleared as soon as I fell. Five minutes later and I would have seen the danger.'

We were now faced with a very dangerous ridge which, although it had collapsed, was no safer as a result. We could see secondary fracture lines in the snow just back from the edge, and one particular fracture ran parallel to and only four feet away from the crest for as far as we could see.

4

ON THE EDGE

There was no question of traversing lower down on the East Face for this was a continuous series of large flutings running down into the clouds which had closed over the void again several hundred feet below us. It had stopped snowing. The flutings would be impossibly slow and dangerous to climb across, and to descend lower would see us lost in the white-out conditions below the cloud. There were few choices left open to us. Simon stood up and began moving gingerly along the crest five feet from the edge, along the continual crack-line running away from us. I moved further down the East Face to wait until he had taken out all the slack rope. At least then I could stop him if the ridge broke away again, but eventually I would have to join him, and we would move together along the ridge.

As I climbed up to rejoin his tracks it occurred to me that I had felt a moment of anxiety only minutes before Simon had fallen. I had noticed this in the past and always wondered about it. There had been no good reason for the sudden stab of worry. We had been on the mountain for over fifty hours and perhaps had become attuned to potential threats; so much so that I had sensed something would happen without understanding quite what it would be. I didn't like this irrational theory, since anxiety had returned with a vengeance. I could see that Simon had also tensed up. The descent was already far more serious than we had reckoned.

I moved carefully. I watched the crack-line, checked I had put my feet exactly where Simon's footsteps were, and continued nervously 150 feet behind Simon, who had his back to me. I might have a chance if I saw him fall in time. I could throw myself down the opposite side of the ridge and expect the ropes to stop us as they sawed through the ridge. He would have little or no warning. He might hear me scream out, or hear the ridge break, but he would have to turn round to see which side I was falling down before he could jump to the safe side. It seemed to me that the most likely accident would involve the whole ridge collapsing, taking us both down in one very long breakaway of snow.

I saw the crack close up, and when I moved past it I breathed a sigh of relief. The ridge was slightly safer at last. Unfortunately it now dropped away steeply and twisted back on itself with each turn, huge cornices bulging out over the West Face. I saw that these difficulties eased further in the distance so I wasn't surprised when Simon began descending the East Face. He intended to lose enough height to be able to traverse directly across to the easier section and avoid descending the tortured ridge. The easier ground lay a couple of hundred feet below our point on the ridge. I guessed how far we needed to descend before following Simon down.

We hadn't descended far before I realised how poor the light had become. I checked my watch and was surprised to see that it had gone five o'clock. We had left the summit nearly three and a half hours earlier and yet had made little progress along the ridge. It would be dark in an hour and, to make things more difficult, the storm clouds had boiled over us again and snowflakes were blowing up from the east into our faces. The temperature had also dropped sharply and, with the wind building up, it felt icy cold whenever we stopped.

Simon descended a gully between two flutings. I followed slowly, trying to keep the distance between us by moving only when the ropes moved. I descended into a uniform whiteness, snow and cloud merging into one. After a while I decided that we must have reached a point where we could now traverse horizontally across to the easier ground, but Simon carried on down. I shouted for him to stop, but received only a muffled reply. I yelled louder and the ropes stopped moving through my gloves. Neither of us could understand the other's shouts, so I moved down to get within earshot. I was alarmed to find that the gully became steeper and I kept slipping. I turned round to face into the slope, but it was still hard to remain in control.

I was close to him when I heard Simon shout again and could hear his query about why we had stopped. At that moment the snow whooshed away from under my feet and I dropped swiftly. I had both axes dug deep into the gully but they didn't stop me. I screamed a warning, and suddenly bumped heavily against Simon, stopping jammed up against him.

'Jesus! . . . I . . . Oh shit! I thought we'd had it . . . this is fucking stupid!'

Simon said nothing. I leant face first into the gully and tried to calm down. My heart seemed to be trying to hammer its way out of my chest, and my legs shook weakly. It had been fortunate that I was so close to Simon when I fell, not too far above to have built up enough speed to knock him down.

'You okay?' Simon asked.

'Yes. Scared . . . that's all.'

'Yeah.'

'We've gone far too low.'

'Oh! I was thinking perhaps we could descend all the way into the eastern glacier bay.'

'You're joking! Bloody hell! I've just nearly killed both of us on this bit, and we haven't a clue what it's like below us.'

'But that ridge is crazy. We'll never get down it tonight.'

'We're not getting off this tonight, anyway. For God's sake, it's almost dark now. If we rush off down there we'll be lucky if we ever get off this bloody thing.'

'Okay . . . okay, calm down. It was just an idea.'

'Sorry. I was freaked out. Couldn't we traverse out sideways from here and get back to the ridge where it drops down?'

'Okay. . . you first.'

I sorted out the tangles from my fall and then began digging into the right side of the fluting. An hour and a half later I had managed to cross innumerable flutings and gullies, and Simon was following a rope's-length behind me. We had covered less than 200 feet, and by then it was snowing hard, bitterly cold and windy. It was also dark and we were having to use our head-torches.

Stumbling through a wall of sugary snow and into another gully, I kicked against rock beneath the snow.

'Simon!' I shouted. 'Stop where you are a while. There's a small rock wall here. It's a bit tricky getting round it.'

I decided to place a rock peg in the wall, and then tentatively balance round the obstacle. I succeeded with the rock peg but somehow managed to fall down and round the wall without coming on to the rope. Simon employed an equally basic climbing technique using gravity and body weight, jumping down the wall without being able to see where he would land, but correct in the assumption that, when he did, it would be with such force that he would safely bury himself firmly in the loose snow beyond. The only flaw I could find in his reasoning was that he didn't know whether his landing would be loose snow or rock! We were too tired and cold by then to care.

Once beyond the rock we crossed an open slope of powder, mercifully without flutings. We were heading back up towards where we guessed the ridge would be, and after a couple of rope-lengths found a large cone of snow swept up against a rock wall. We decided to dig a snow cave.

Simon's head-torch kept flickering from a loose or damaged connection. I began digging and soon struck rock. I tried digging parallel with the rock, to make a long narrow cave, but after half an hour gave up. The cave had so many holes in it that it would provide little protection from the wind. It was bitterly cold, and Simon had struggled to repair his head-torch with his bare fingers, fiddling with the copper contacts in the dark. Digging had kept me warm, despite the temperature falling to around the minus twenty mark, but two of Simon's fingers were frostbitten. He became angry with me when I started to dig another cave. Unjustly, I decided that Simon was behaving petulantly and ignored him. The next site for the cave was marginally better and although I struck rock I managed to build it to fit the two of us. By then Simon had mended the torch but his fingers were beyond rewarming. He was still bristling with anger at my lack of co-operation.

I prepared the meal. There was little enough left. We ate chocolate and dried fruit and drank a lot of fruit juice. By then we had forgotten our tired anger and regained a sense of perspective. I had been as cold and tired as Simon, and had only wanted a cave dug quickly so that we could get into our sleeping bags and make some hot drinks. It had been another very long day. It had started well, and we had been glad to get off the West Face, but the descent had become increasingly difficult and nerve-wracking. Falling over the cornice had shaken both of us, and the strain afterwards had been wearing. We had got angry enough with each other today, and more of the same wouldn't help.

Simon showed me his fingers, which had slowly come back to life. But the index finger on each hand remained white and solid as far back as the first knuckle. So, he had frostbite. I hoped it would not suffer further damage the next day. However, I felt sure that we were close to the end of the difficulties on the ridge, and that we would be able to reach base camp by the following afternoon. We only had enough gas left for two drinks in the morning, but that should be enough. As I settled myself down for sleep I couldn't shake off the dread feelings I had experienced while traversing the ridge. The image of the two of us falling helplessly down the East Face, still roped together, had all too nearly come true. I shuddered at the prospect of such an end. I knew Simon must have felt the same. The year before he had witnessed just such a terrible accident at the Croz Spur, high in the Mont Blanc range of the French Alps. Two Japanese climbers had fallen to their deaths from close to where he stood, only a short distance from the top of the route.

For three days stormy weather had produced atrocious conditions. The rocks were plastered in verglas, a hard patina of ice covering the holds and filling the cracks. Progress had been painfully slow as each hold was chipped clear, and otherwise easy sections had become desperately extreme climbing. Simon and his partner, Jon Sylvester, had bivouacked twice on the face, and late in the afternoon of that third day, another storm was building up – the temperature plummeting, heavy clouds shrouding them in a world of their own, and the first spindrift powder snow avalanches sweeping down.

The two Japanese climbers had been following them closely. They had bivouacked separately, and there was no communication between the two teams, nor was there any sense of competitiveness or a suggestion that they might join forces. Both parties were coping equally well in the difficult conditions. There were frequent falls, often from the same points. They had watched one another struggle, fall, and try again as they progressed up the face.

When they reached the summit headwall Simon had seen the leading Japanese climber fall outwards and backwards, arms outstretched in surprise. The awesome 2,500-foot plunge, visible through breaks in the cloud, was framed behind him. To his horror, he had then seen the falling leader jerk and twist and, without a sound, pull his partner into the void. Their belay piton had torn free. The two men plunged down, roped together, helpless.

Simon had struggled up to Jon's stance, which was out of sight of that lower section, and told him what had happened. They stood quietly on the small rock ledge in the gathering storm trying to absorb the enormity of what had just taken place so close to them. There was nothing they could do for the two men, who would never have survived the fall, and the quickest way to get news to the rescue services would be over the summit and down into Italy.

As they resumed the climb they were shocked to hear a ghastly screaming from far below – the chilling sounds of someone in agony, desperately alone and terrified. Looking down, they saw the two climbers sliding down the upper icefield at ever-increasing speed 600 feet below them. They were still roped together, and various scattered items of gear and their rucksacks tumbled alongside them. All Simon could do was to stare helplessly at the two tiny figures racing down the ice. Then they were gone: disappearing over the lip of the icefield, falling out of view into the horrendous drop to the glacier.

By some desperate quirk at least one of the climbers must have survived the initial fall on to the icefield. Somehow they had been stopped, probably with their rope snagged on some rocky projection – but they weren't saved. It was a cruel twist, both for the victims and for the horrified spectators far above them. Only a short reprieve, five minutes or so, while one of them fought to make himself safe and find some anchor. Badly injured, he had had little chance. Perhaps he had slipped, or the rope had unsnagged: whatever had happened, the outcome was brutally final.

Simon and Jon, their confidence shattered, minds numbed by it all, had turned and struggled on up to the summit. It had been so sudden. They hadn't conversed with the two Japanese, but a mutual understanding and respect had developed. If they had all got down safely, then they would have talked, shared food on the long walk to the valley, met up in a bar in town, perhaps become friends.

I could remember seeing Simon walking slowly into the camp-site outside Chamonix when he got back. He was subdued and looked drawn and tired. He had sat numb, repeatedly questioning why his own tumble had been held on the same piton just before the Japanese leader had fallen and ripped it out. A day later he was his normal self again: an experience absorbed, shelved in his memory, understood and accepted, and left at that.

As sleep crept swiftly through me I tried to shake off the thought of how close we had come to the same appalling end as those two Japanese. There would have been no one to watch us, I thought: as if it would have made any difference.

I had the stove burning away cheerfully by my side, and could look beyond it through a hole in the snow cave. The East Face of Yerupaja was framed perfectly in the circular window I had accidentally built into the cave. The early-morning sun etched the ridge lines with shadows, and danced blue shadings down the edges of the flutings on the face. For the first time in the last four days the tense concentration in my body relaxed. The anxious struggles of the previous night had been forgotten, and the memory of how close we had come to falling to our deaths had faded. I gave myself time to enjoy where I was, and to congratulate myself. I craved a cigarette.

It was cramped in the snow hole, but infinitely warmer than in the previous one. Simon was still asleep, lying on his side close by me, facing away. His hips and shoulders pressed up against my side, and I could feel his body warmth seeping through my sleeping bag. The close intimacy seemed odd despite how together we had been on the mountain. I moved carefully to avoid waking him. I looked through the round hole window at the East Face and felt myself smiling. I knew it would be a good day.

The gas was all used up in the breakfast routine and there would be no more water until we got down to the lakes below the moraines. I dressed and geared up first, before climbing out of the cave and going over to the first cave I had attempted to dig. Simon was slow getting ready, and it wasn't until he joined me on the large platform of the collapsed cave that I remembered his frostbite. My good humour vanished, to be replaced by worry, when he showed his fingers to me. One fingertip was blackened and three other fingers were white and wooden in appearance. Funny how my anxiety seemed to have more to do with whether he would be able to carry on climbing after we got down rather than concern for his injuries.

I started up towards the crest of the ridge which was bathed in sunshine half a rope's-length above me while Simon remained below guarding the ropes. We were both nervous about the possibility of another cornice collapse. When I reached the ridge I was dismayed to see that there was a long section of tortured cornices and knife-edge powder to negotiate. My hope that we might have by-passed it all the day before evaporated. I shouted a warning down to Simon and he agreed to follow me, moving together, once all the rope had run out.

Though we moved with exaggerated caution, we couldn't avoid slipping and falling, only half in control, down the worst sections. I stayed close to the top of the ridge, which kept curling back on itself and dropping suddenly in short steep walls. The possibility of a cornice collapse gradually faded from my mind as I moved, and I became resigned to the helplessness of our situation. The flutings lower down the East Face would almost certainly be a worse proposition. As great a danger as the cornices was the risk of a fall. Any fall requiring a rope to stop it was going to be fatal; neither of us would stand a chance. Yet every time I approached a steep section and was forced to back-climb facing into the snow I usually did so by a combination of falling and climbing. The powder was so insubstantial that, however hard I kicked my legs, I would whoosh down a few feet as soon as I got my weight off my arms. Each sudden heart-stopping slide seemed somehow to halt of its own accord. Where I would stop would be no more solid than where I had fallen from. It wore one's nerves ragged.

I slipped again, but this time yelped out in fright. The short steep slope I was descending bottomed directly on to the edge of the ridge, which had curved back on itself. I had seen as I turned to face into the slope that a huge powdery cornice bulged out beneath this curve, and falling away below it the West Face plunged thousands of feet down to the glacier. Simon, moving a full rope's-length behind me, was out of sight and would have no warning; no idea which side I was falling down. I rushed down in a flurry of powder so fast that my yelp came out more as a squeak of alarm than an attempted warning cry. Simon didn't see the fall, and heard nothing.

Then, just as suddenly, I stopped, with my whole body pressed into the snow, head buried in it, with my arms and legs spreadeagled in a desperate crabbed position. I dared not move. It seemed as if only luck was holding me on to the slope, and feeling the snow moving and sliding down past my stomach and thighs just made me cringe in deeper.

I lifted my head and glanced sideways over my right shoulder. I was on the very edge of the ridge, exactly at the point of the curve. My body was tipped over to the right so that I seemed to be hanging out over the West Face. All my thoughts became locked into not moving. I gasped fast breaths, scared sucks at the air, but I didn't move. When I looked again I realised that I wasn't actually off-balance, although the brief glance before had made me think I was. It was like discovering the trick behind an optical illusion, suddenly seeing what you had really been staring at all the time. The curve of the ridge away back to my left, and the glimpse of the bulging cornice under its arc, had confused me so much that I had thought I was leaning over the fall line. In fact I found that my right leg had punctured straight through the cornice and, though my other leg had stopped me, it had also pushed me over sideways. This explained why I felt unbalanced, right side down. I scrabbled and clawed at the snow on my left, trying to pull my weight over to that side, trying to get my right leg back on to the ridge. Eventually I succeeded and moved away from the edge, following the curve of the ridge again.

Simon appeared above me, moving slowly, looking down at his feet all the time. I had moved to a safer place and shouted a warning for him to descend the slope further to the left, and realised as I did so that I was shaking violently. My legs had gone to sudden jelly, quivering, and it took a long while for the reaction to fade. Long enough for me to watch Simon face into the slope and descend it in two footsteps and the inevitable rushing slide. When he turned and followed my steps I could see the tension in his face. The day was neither enjoyable nor funny, and when he reached me the fear was infectious. We chattered out our alarm in quavery voices; quick staccato curses and repeated phrases tumbling out before we calmed.

5

DISASTER

We had left the snow hole at seven thirty, and two and a half hours later I could see that our progress was painfully slow. Since leaving the summit the previous afternoon we had descended no more than 1,000 feet instead of getting all the way down to the glacier in the six hours which we had reckoned. I began to feel impatient. I was tired of this grinding need to concentrate all the time. The mountain had lost its excitement, its novelty, and I wanted to get off it as soon as possible. The air was bitingly cold and the sky cloudless; the sun burnt down in a dazzling glare on the endless snow and ice. As long as we were back on the glacier before the afternoon storms I didn't care a damn what the weather chose to do.

At last the twisting mayhem of the upper ridge eased, and I could walk upright across the broad level ridge which undulated away in whale-backed humps towards the drop at its northern end. Simon caught up with me as I rested on my sack. We didn't speak. The morning had already taken its toll, and there was nothing left to say. Looking up at our footsteps weaving an unsteady path down towards us, I vowed silently to be more careful about checking descent routes in future.

I shouldered my sack and set off again, with no qualms about being in front now. I had wanted Simon to lead on the last stretch but had been unable to voice my apprehension and feared his response to it more than I feared another sickening fall. Deep snow had built up on the wide, level saddle, and, instead of anxiety swamping my every move I was back to the frustration of wallowing through powder snow.

I had run out the rope, and Simon was getting up to follow when I stepped into the first crevasse.

In a rushing drop, I suddenly found myself standing upright but with my eyes level with the snow. The shallow fissure was filled with powder, so that however hard I thrashed about I seemed to make no upward movement at all. Eventually I managed to haul myself back on to level ground. From a safe distance Simon had watched my struggles with a grin on his face. I moved farther along the ridge and sank down again neck-deep in the snow. I yelled and cursed as I clawed my way back on to the ridge and, by the time I had traversed half-way across the plateau above it, I had fallen into another four small crevasses. However hard I tried, I could not see any tell-tale marks indicating their presence. Simon was following a full rope's-length behind. Frustration and the mounting exhaustion maddened me to a fury which I knew would be vented on Simon if he came close enough.

Then, crouching beside the hole I had just made, trying to regain my breath, I glanced back and was shocked to see clear through the ridge into the yawning abyss below. Blue-white light gleamed up through the hole from the expanse of the West Face, which I could see looming beneath it. Suddenly it clicked in my brain why I had fallen through so many times. It was all one crevasse, one long fracture line cutting right through the enormous humping cornices that made up the plateau. I moved quickly away to the side and shouted a warning to Simon. The rolling ridge had been so wide and flat it had never occurred to me that we might actually be standing on an overhanging cornice, one as large as the summit cornice, but stretching for several hundred feet. If it had collapsed we would have gone with it.

I kept well back from the edge after that, leaving a healthy margin of fifty feet. Simon had fallen with the smaller cornice collapse when he was forty feet back from the edge. There was no point in taking chances now that the flutings on the east side had eased into a uniformly smooth slope. My legs felt leaden trudging through the deep snow towards the end of the plateau. As I crested the last rise in the ridge and glanced back, I saw Simon hauling himself along in the same head-down, dog-tired manner as myself, a full rope's-length from me, 150 feet away, and I knew he would be out of sight once I began descending the long easy-angled slope ahead.

I had hoped to see the slope run down to the col but was disappointed to find it rising slightly to a minor summit of cornices before dropping steeply down again. Even so, I could see enough of the South Ridge of Yerupaja to know that the col would certainly lie immediately below that next drop, and then we would be at the lowest point on the ridge connecting Yerupaja and Siula Grande. Another half-hour would put us on that col, and it would be easy going from there to the glacier. I perked up.

Starting down, I felt at once the change in angle. It was so much easier than the plod along the saddle, and I would have romped happily down the gentle slope but for the rope tugging insistently at my waist. I had forgotten that Simon would still be wearily following my tracks on the saddle.

I had expected to be able to take a direct line to the small rise without encountering any obstacles, and was surprised to find that the slope ended abruptly in an ice cliff. It cut right across my path at right-angles, bisecting the ridge. I approached the edge cautiously and peered over a twenty-five-foot drop. The slope at its base swept down to the right in a smooth, steeply angled face. Beyond that lay the last rise on the ridge, about 200 feet away. The height of the cliff increased rapidly as it cut away from the ridge. I stood roughly mid-point on this wedge of ice running across the ridge, with its narrow edge abutting the ridge line. I traversed carefully away from the ridge, occasionally looking over the cliff to see if there was any weakness in the wall, which stood thirty-five feet high at its end. I had already discounted the possibility of abseiling past the cliff, for the snow at the top of the cliff was too loose to take an ice stake.

There were two options open to me. Either I could stay on the ridge top or I could continue away from it and hope to by-pass the steep section by a wide descending traverse. From where I stood at the end of the cliff I could see that this would be very tiring and risky. We would have to detour in a wide arc down, across, and then back up again, to by-pass the cliff. The initial slope down looked very steep and very unstable. I had had enough of slip-sliding around this ridge, and the empty sweep thousands of feet into the eastern glacier bay below the slope nudged me into decision. If either of us fell we would be on open slopes. We wouldn't stop. At least on the ridge we had been able to kid ourselves that we could, with luck, jump either side of the apex in the event of a fall.

I retraced my steps, intending to climb down the cliff at the easiest point. I knew this would be impossible near the crest of the ridge since there it was a near-vertical wall of powder snow. I needed to find a weakness in the cliff, a ramp line or a crevasse running down the cliff to give me some purchase on the ice, which appeared solid to within a few yards of the edge of the ridge. At last I saw what I was looking for – a very slight break in the angle of the ice wall. This part of the cliff was still steep, nearly vertical, but not quite. It was about twenty feet high at the break and I felt sure that at this point a few quick moves of reverse climbing would see me past the problem.

Crouching down on my knees, I turned my back to the cliff edge and managed to get my axes to bite in deeply. Slowly, I lowered my legs over the cliff until the edge was against my stomach and I could kick my crampons into the ice wall below me. I felt them bite and hold. Removing one axe, I hammered it in again very close to the edge. It held fast and solid. I removed my ice hammer and lowered my chest and shoulders over the edge until I could see the ice wall and swing at it with the hammer. I was hanging on to the ice axe, reaching to my side to place the hammer solidly into the wall with my left hand. I got it to bite after a few blows but wasn't happy about it and removed it to try again. I wanted it to be perfect before I removed the axe embedded in the lip and lowered myself on to the hammer. As the hammer came out there was a sharp cracking sound and my right hand, gripping

71

the axe, pulled down. The sudden jerk turned me outwards and instantly I was falling.

I hit the slope at the base of the cliff before I saw it coming. I was facing into the slope and both knees locked as I struck it. I felt a shattering blow in my knee, felt bones splitting, and screamed. The impact catapulted me over backwards and down the slope of the East Face. I slid, head-first, on my back. The rushing speed of it confused me. I thought of the drop below but felt nothing. Simon would be ripped off the mountain. He couldn't hold this. I screamed again as I jerked to a sudden violent stop.

Everything was still, silent. My thoughts raced madly. Then pain flooded down my thigh – a fierce burning fire coming down the inside of my thigh, seeming to ball in my groin, building and building until I cried out at it, and my breathing came in ragged gasps. My leg! Oh Jesus. My leg!

I hung, head down, on my back, left leg tangled in the rope above me and my right leg hanging slackly to one side. I lifted my head from the snow and stared, up across my chest, at a grotesque distortion in the right knee, twisting the leg into a strange zigzag. I didn't connect it with the pain which burnt my groin. That had nothing to do with my knee. I kicked my left leg free of the rope and swung round until I was hanging against the snow on my chest, feet down. The pain eased. I kicked my left foot into the slope and stood up.

A wave of nausea surged over me. I pressed my face into the snow, and the sharp cold seemed to calm me. Something terrible, something dark with dread occurred to me, and as I thought about it I felt the dark thought break into panic: 'I've broken my leg, that's it. I'm dead. Everyone said it . . . if there's just two of you a broken ankle could turn into a death sentence . . . if it's broken . . . if . . . It doesn't hurt so much, maybe I've just ripped something.'

I kicked my right leg against the slope, feeling sure it wasn't broken. My knee exploded. Bone grated, and the fireball rushed from groin to knee. I screamed. I looked down at the knee and could see it was broken, yet I tried not to believe what I was seeing. It wasn't just broken, it was ruptured, twisted, crushed, and I could see the kink in the joint and knew what had happened. The impact had driven my lower leg up through the knee joint.

Oddly enough, looking at it seemed to help. I felt detached from it, as if I were making a clinical observation of someone else. I moved the knee gingerly, experimenting with it. I tried to bend it and stopped immediately, gasping at the rush of pain. When it moved I felt a grinding crunch; bone had moved, and a lot more besides. At least it wasn't an open fracture. I knew this as soon as I tried to move. I could feel no wetness, no blood. I reached down and caressed the knee with my right hand, trying to ignore the stabs of fire, so that I could feel it with enough force to be certain I wasn't bleeding. It was in one solid piece, but it felt huge, and twisted – and not mine. The pain kept flooding round it, pouring on fire, as if that might cure it then and there.

With a groan I squeezed my eyes tight shut. Hot tears filled my eyes and my contact lenses swam in them. I squeezed tight again and felt hot drops rolling over my face. It wasn't the pain, I felt sorry for myself, childishly so, and with that thought I couldn't help the tears. Dying had seemed so far away, and yet now everything was tinged with it. I shook my head to stop the tears, but the taint was still there.

I dug my axes into the snow, and pounded my good leg deeply into the soft slope until I felt sure it wouldn't slip. The effort brought back the nausea and I felt my head spin giddily to the point of fainting. I moved and a searing spasm of pain cleared away the faintness. I could see the summit of Seria Norte away to the west. I was not far below it. The sight drove home how desperately things had changed. We were above 19,000 feet, still on the ridge, and very much alone. I looked south at the small rise I had hoped to scale quickly and it seemed to grow with every second that I stared. I would never get over it. Simon would not be able to get me up it. He would leave me. He had no choice. I held my breath, thinking about it. Left here? Alone? I felt cold at the thought. I remembered Rob, who had been left to die . . . but Rob had been unconscious, had been dying. I had only a bad leg.

Nothing to kill me. For an age I felt overwhelmed at the notion of being left; I felt like screaming, and I felt like swearing, but stayed silent. If I said a word I would panic. I could feel myself teetering on the edge of it.

The rope which had been tight on my harness went slack. Simon was coming! He must know something had happened, I thought, but what shall I tell him? If I told him that I had only hurt my leg and not broken it, would that make him help me? My mind raced at the prospect of telling him that I was hurt. I pressed my face into the cold snow again and tried to think calmly. I had to cool it. If he saw me panicky and hysterical he might give up at once. I fought to stem my fears. Be rational about it, I thought. I felt myself calm down, and my breathing became steady; even the pain seemed tolerable.

'What happened? Are you okay?'

I looked up in surprise. I hadn't heard his approach. He stood at the top of the cliff looking down at me, puzzled. I made an effort to talk normally, as if nothing had happened:

'I fell. The edge gave way.' I paused, then I said as unemotionally as I could: 'I've broken my leg.'

His expression changed instantly. I could see a whole range of reactions in his face. I kept looking directly at him. I wanted to miss nothing.

'Are you sure it's broken?'

'Yes.'

He stared at me. It seemed that he looked harder and longer than he should have done because he turned away sharply. Not sharply enough though. I had seen the look come across his face briefly, but in that instant I knew his thoughts. He had an odd air of detachment. I felt unnerved by it, felt suddenly quite different from him, alienated. His eyes had been full of thoughts. Pity. Pity and something else; a distance given to a wounded animal which could not be helped. He had tried to hide it, but I had seen in, and I looked away full of dread and worry.

'I'll abseil down to you.'

He had his back to me, bending over a snow stake, digging down through the soft snow. He sounded matter-of-fact, and

74

I wondered whether I was being unduly paranoid. I waited for him to say more, but he remained silent and I wondered what he was thinking. A short but very dangerous abseil from a poorly anchored snow stake put him down next to me quickly.

He stood close by me and said nothing. I had seen him glance at my leg but he made no comment. After some searching he found a packet of Paracetamols and handed me two pills. I swallowed them, and watched him trying to pull the abseil rope down. It refused to move. It had jammed in the snow bollard that he had dug around the snow stake above. Simon swore and set off towards the point where the wall was smallest, right on the crest of the ridge. I knew it was all unstable powder and so did he, but he had no choice. I looked away, unwilling to watch what I was sure would be a fatal fall down the West Face. Indirectly it would kill me as well, only a little more slowly.

Simon had said nothing about what he would do, and I had been nervous to prompt him. In an instant an uncrossable gap had come between us and we were no longer a team working together.

Joe had disappeared behind a rise in the ridge and began moving faster than I could go. I was glad we had put the steep section behind us at last. I had felt so close to the end of everything on that ridge. Falling all the time and always on the very edge of the West Face. I felt tired and was grateful to be able to follow Joe's tracks instead of breaking trail.

I rested a while when I saw that Joe had stopped moving. Obviously he had found an obstacle and I thought I would wait until he started moving again. When the rope moved again I trudged forward after it, slowly.

Suddenly there was a sharp tug as the rope lashed out taut across the slope. I was pulled forward several feet as I pushed my axes into the snow and braced myself for another jerk. Nothing happened. I knew that Joe had fallen, but I couldn't see him, so I stayed put. I waited for about ten minutes until the tautened rope went slack on the snow and I felt sure that

Joe had got his weight off me. I began to move along his footsteps cautiously, half expecting something else to happen. I kept tensed up and ready to dig my axes in at the first sign of trouble.

As I crested the rise, I could see down a slope to where the rope disappeared over the edge of a drop. I approached slowly, wondering what had happened. When I reached the top of the drop I saw Joe below me. He had one foot dug in and was leaning against the slope with his face buried in the snow. I asked him what had happened and he looked at me in surprise. I knew he was injured, but the significance didn't hit me at first.

He told me very calmly that he had broken his leg. He looked pathetic, and my immediate thought came without any emotion, You're fucked, matey. You're dead . . . no two ways about it! I think he knew it too. I could see it in his face. It was all totally rational. I knew where we were, I took in everything around me instantly, and knew he was dead. It never occurred to me that I might also die. I accepted without question that I could get off the mountain alone. I had no doubt about that.

I saw what Joe had tried to do and realised that, unless I could arrange an abseil, I would have to do the same. The snow at the top of the cliff was horrendous sugary stuff. I dug as much of the surface away as I could and then buried a snow stake in the mush I had uncovered. I felt sure it would never hold my weight so I started digging a wide snow bollard around the stake. When I finished I backed towards the cliff edge and tugged the rope. It held firm but I had no confidence in it. I thought of trying to back-climb the crest of the ridge where the cliff was smallest but decided it would be even more dangerous. I half-abseiled and half-climbed down the cliff, trying to get my weight off the rope. I felt it cutting through the bollard. It held firm.

When I reached the foot of the cliff I saw that Joe's leg was in a bad way and that he was suffering. He seemed calm but had a sort of hunted, fearful look in his eyes. He knew the score as well as I did. I gave him some pills for the pain but knew they were not strong enough to help much. His leg was twisted and misshapen at the knee joint, and I thought that if I could see that through his thick polar-fibre trousers then it must be really bad.

I was at a loss for something to say. The change in our fortunes was too abrupt. I found that the ropes had jammed and knew I would have to go back up, alone, to free them. In a way, it took my mind off things, and gave me time to settle into the new situation. I had to solo back up the cliff, and the only way was right on the crest of the ridge. I was frightened of attempting it. Joe tried moving beside me and very nearly fell off. I grabbed him and put him back into balance. He stayed silent. He had unroped so I had been able to arrange the abseil and I think he was quiet because he knew that if I hadn't grabbed him he would have fallen the length of the East Face. I left him then, and forgot about him.

The climb up the edge of the cliff was the hardest and most dangerous thing I'd ever done. Several times my leg broke through the powder into space. When I was half-way up I realised I couldn't go back, but I didn't think I would get up it. I seemed to be climbing on nothing. Everything I touched simply broke away. Every step either sank back, collapsed or crumbled down the West Face, but incredibly I seemed to be gaining height. I don't know how long it took. It felt like hours. When eventually I pulled myself on to the slope above I was shaking and so strung out that I had to stop still and calm myself.

I looked back and was amazed to see that Joe had started traversing away from the cliff. He was trying to help himself by contouring round the small rise in front of him. He moved so slowly, planting his axes in deeply until his arms were buried and then making a frightening little hop sideways. He shuffled across the slope, head down, completely enclosed in his own private struggle. Below him I could see thousands of feet of open face falling into the eastern glacier bay. I watched him quite dispassionately. I couldn't help him, and it occurred to me that in all likelihood he would fall to his death. I wasn't disturbed by the thought. In a way I hoped he would fall. I *knew I couldn't leave him while he was still fighting for it, but I had no idea how I might help him. I could get down. If I tried to get him down I might die with him. It didn't frighten me. It just seemed a waste. It would be pointless. I kept staring at him expecting him to fall . . .*

After a long wait I turned and went up to the snow stake. I rearranged the stake and then backed down to the cliff edge again. I prayed it would hold me, and when I touched down on the slope below prayed again that it wouldn't jam. I had no intention of repeating the climb up the crest. The rope slid down easily and I turned with it, half-expecting to see that Joe had gone. He was still climbing away from me. In all the time it had taken me to get up and down he had covered only 100 feet. I started after him.

Simon suddenly appeared at my side. I had been unable to watch him climbing the crest. I felt sure he would fall. Instead, I thought, I had better try to get moving. I knew I would never get over the rise, so I began to contour it. I didn't think of the consequences. I had seen Simon struggling on the powder. Progress was slow and tiring, but I was so focused in on moving carefully that I could ignore much of the pain. It became one more difficulty to contend with and merged with all the other problems – balance, the snow conditions and one-leggedness.

A pattern of movements developed after my initial wobbly hops and I meticulously repeated the pattern. Each pattern made up one step across the slope and I began to feel detached from everything around me. I thought of nothing but the patterns. Only once did I stop and glance back at Simon. He seemed to be on the very point of falling and I looked away quickly. I could see the endless fall of the East Face beneath my feet. It was tempting to think I could survive falling down it, yet I knew that despite there being evenly angled snow all the way, the speed of the fall would rip me to shreds long before I reached the bottom. I thought of falling down it anyway, but it meant nothing to me. I felt no fright at the idea. It seemed such an obvious and unavoidable fact. It was academic really. I knew I was done for. It would make no difference in the long run.

Simon climbed past me and began stamping a trench across the slope until he had gone out of sight round the curve of the slope. He said he was going ahead to see what lay around the corner. Neither of us discussed what we were going to do. I don't think we thought there was anything. So I got back into my patterns. The trench made it easier, but it still needed total attention. It struck me that we were both avoiding the issue. For over two hours we had acted as if nothing had happened. We had a silent agreement. It needed time to work itself out. We both knew the truth; it was very simple. I was injured and unlikely to survive. Simon could get down alone. While I waited on his actions, it felt as if I was holding something terrifyingly fragile and precious. If I asked Simon to help, I might lose this precious thing. He might leave me. I remained silent, but it was no longer for fear of losing control. I felt coldly rational.

The patterns merged into automatic rhythm. I was surprised to hear Simon ask if I was all right. I had forgotten about him, and had no idea how long I had been repeating the patterns; I had almost forgotten why I was doing them. I looked up and saw Simon sitting in the snow watching me. I smiled at him and he returned a lopsided sort of grin which failed to mask his anxiety. He sat overlooking the slope running down the side of the rise round which we had contoured. Behind him I could see the crest of the ridge.

'I can see the col,' he said, and I felt a surge of hope run through me like a cold wind.

'Is it clear? I mean, is it a straight slope down?' I asked, trying to keep the edge of excitement from my voice.

'More or less . . .'

I hurried my patterned moves, and at the same time tried not to rush. Suddenly I was scared of the drop below. I could feel myself trembling and realised that if I had felt like this when I had set out I would never have got to this point. When I reached him, I slumped against the snow.

Simon put his hand on my shoulder. 'How're you doing?'

'It's better. Painful, but . . .' I felt small and useless telling him. His concern scared me, and I was unsure what was behind it. Perhaps he wanted to break the news to me softly. 'I've had it, Simon . . . I can't see myself getting down at this rate.'

If I expected an answer I didn't get one. It felt melodramatic to have voiced it, and he ignored the implied question. He began untying the ropes from his harness.

I looked down to the col. It was about 600 feet below us and slightly to the right. Without thinking, I began to work out possible ways of getting to it. To descend directly to the col would be very difficult since it meant a diagonal descent crossing the angle of the slope. It would have to be straight down and then horizontally across to the col. The traverse appeared shorter than the slope I'd just crossed.

'Do you think you can hold my weight in this snow?' I asked.

We had no snow stakes left. If Simon took my weight on the rope, he would have to do so standing on the loose open slope with no anchors.

'If we dig a big bucket seat I should be able to hold you. If it starts to collapse I can always shout, and you can take your weight off.'

'Okay. It would be quicker if you lowered me on two ropes tied together.'

He nodded in agreement. Already he had begun to dig out his belay seat. I grabbed the two ropes, knotted them together and tied myself into the free end. The other end was already attached to Simon's harness. In effect we were now roped together with one 300-foot line, which would halve the time spent digging belay seats and double the distance lowered. Simon could control the speed of my descent by using a belay plate, and so reduce any sudden jerks of weight and avoid having the rope run away from him if he couldn't get a grip on it with his frozen mitts. The one problem was the knot joining the two ropes. The only way to get it past the belay plate would be by disconnecting the rope from the plate and then reconnecting it with the knot on the other side. This would be possible only if I stood up and took my weight off the rope. I thanked my stars that I hadn't broken both legs.

'Okay. You ready?'

Simon was seated in the deep hole he had dug in the slope, with his legs braced hard into the snow. He held the belay plate locked off with the rope to me taut between us.

'Yes. Now take it steady. If anything slips, yell.'

'Don't worry, I will. If you can't hear me when the knot comes up, I'll tug the ropes three times.'

'Right.'

I lay on my chest immediately beneath Simon, and edged down until all my weight was on the rope. Initially I couldn't commit myself to letting my feet hang free of the snow. If the seat crumbled straight away we would be falling instantaneously. Simon nodded at me and grinned. Encouraged by his confidence I lifted my feet and began to slide down. It worked!

He let the rope out smoothly in a steady descent. I lay against the snow holding an axe in each hand ready to dig them in the moment I felt a fall begin. Occasionally the crampons on my right boot snagged in the snow and jarred my leg. I tried not to cry out but failed. I didn't want Simon to stop.

In a surprisingly short time he did stop. I looked up and saw that he had receded far from me, and I could make out only his head and shoulders leaning out from the seat in the snow. He shouted something but I couldn't make it out until three sharp tugs explained it. After the endless time traversing the rise I was astounded at the speed at which I had descended 150 feet. Astounded and pleased as punch, I wanted to giggle. In so short a time my mood had swung from despair to wild optimism, and death rushed back to being a vague possibility rather than the inevitable fact. The rope went slack as I hopped up on to my good leg. I was acutely aware that while Simon was changing the knot over we were at our most vulnerable. If I fell, I would drop a whole rope's length before it came tight on to him, and he would be whipped off the mountain by the impact. I dug my axes in and stayed motionless. I could see the col below and to my right, already a lot closer. More tugs on the rope and I carefully leant my body down the slope as the second half of the lower began.

I waved up at the distant red and blue dot above me and saw him stand up out of the seat. He turned and faced into the slope and began kicking his feet into the snow. The rope curled down past me. Simon was on his way down. I turned and started to excavate another seat. I dug deep into the slope, making a hole that he could sit completely inside. I curved the back wall and the floor so that it rose up to the lip of the hole. When satisfied, I looked back up to see Simon back-climbing quickly towards me.

The next lowering was much quicker. We had adopted an efficient system. One shadow lay over our building optimism – the weather. It had deteriorated rapidly, clouds flitting across the col, and a great mass of cloud boiling up in the east. The wind was increasing steadily, blowing powder snow across the slope. I could see plumes of snow streaming horizontally out over the West Face. As the wind grew, so the temperature dropped. I could feel it burning into my face, numbing my chin and nose. My fingers began to freeze.

Simon joined me at the end of the second lowering. We were almost level with the col but there was a horizontal traverse to be made to get to its edge.

'I'll go ahead and make a trench.'

He didn't wait for an answer, and I felt exposed as I watched him move away from me. It looked a long way to the col. I wondered whether to unrope. I didn't want to, even though logic told me the rope wouldn't save me now. If I fell I would take Simon with me, but I couldn't bring myself to dispense with the comforting reassurance of the rope. I glanced at Simon. I couldn't believe it! He had reached the col yet he was only about eighty feet from me. The late-afternoon light had disguised the distance.

'Come on!' he shouted above the wind. 'I've got the rope.'

There was a gentle tug at my waist. He had taken in the remaining slack and intended belaying me. I thought that he meant to jump down the west side if I fell. There was no other way of stopping me. I hobbled sideways and nearly lost balance as I snagged my foot. Something gristly twisted in my knee, and the shock had me sobbing. It eased away and I swore at myself for not concentrating. The crabbed sideways pattern of movement which I had tried before took over once more. When I couldn't swing my leg across I reached down and hefted it along the trench Simon had forged, and then returned to my patterns. The leg had become inanimate, a weighty useless object. If it got in my way, or pained me, I cursed it and hefted it aside as if it were a chair I had tripped over.

The col was exposed and windy, but for the first time we could see clearly down the west flank of the mountain. Directly beneath us the glacier we had walked up five days ago curved away towards the moraines and crevasses which led to base camp, nearly 3,000 feet below us. It would take many long lowerings, but it was all downhill, and we had lost the sense of hopelessness that had invaded us at the ice cliff. Reaching the col had been crucial. If there had been any steep ground between the cliff and the col we would never have got past it.

'What time is it?' Simon asked.

'Just gone four. We don't have much time, do we?'

I could see him weighing up the possibilities. The face below the col was running with spindrift, and the cloud buildup was nearly complete. It was hard to judge whether it had started snowing because of the powder being swept against us by the wind. We hadn't sat on the col for very long, yet already I was numb with cold. I wanted to carry on down but it was Simon's decision. I waited for him to make up his mind.

'I think we should keep going,' he said at last. 'Will you be all right?'

'Yes. Let's go. I'm freezing.'

'Me too. My hands have gone again.'

'We could snow-hole if you like.'

'No. We won't reach the glacier in the light, but it's a clear slope down. Better to lose height.'

'Right. I don't like the look of this weather.'

'That's what worries me. Okay, I'll lower you from here. We should go down further to the right but I don't think you will be able to make it diagonally. We'll just have to take our chances straight down.'

I slid off the crest of the ridge and down the West Face. Simon stood back from the edge, bracing himself against my weight. The first of many powder avalanches rushed over me, tugging me down. I slid faster, and shouted to Simon to slow down, but he couldn't hear me.

6

THE FINAL CHOICE

I dug the bucket seat with frantic and nervous haste. The first lowering 300 feet down from the col had worried me. It had been quite impossible to descend in a diagonal line to the right. Gravity had turned me into a dead weight and no amount of scrabbling against the snow with ice axes had prevented a plumb vertical descent.

The conditions on the face were markedly different from those on the slopes above the col. Simon let me slide faster than I had expected and, despite my cries of alarm and pain, he had kept the pace of descent going. I stopped shouting to him after fifty feet. The rising wind and continuous spindrift avalanches drowned out all communications. Instead I concentrated on keeping my leg clear of the snow. It was an impossible task. Despite lying on my good leg, the crampons on the right boot snagged in the snow as the weight of my body pushed down. Each abrupt jerk caused searing pain in my knee. I sobbed and gasped, swore at the snow and the cold, and most of all at Simon. At the change-over point, I hopped on to my left leg after feeling the tugs on the rope and hammering the axe shafts into the snow, bent over them, trying to think the pain away. It ebbed slowly, leaving a dreadful throbbing ache and a leaden tiredness.

The tugs came again far too soon, and carelessly I slumped against the rope and let myself go. The drop went on until I could bear it no longer, yet there was nothing that I could do to bring the agony to an end. Howling and screaming for Simon to stop achieved nothing; the blame had to lie somewhere, so I swore Simon's character to the devil. I kept thinking the rope must come to an end, that I would stop at any moment, but it seemed to have doubled in length.

The face here was much steeper than above the col, steep enough to frighten me, and make me think that Simon was barely in control. I couldn't ignore the thought of his seat collapsing and tensed up. I waited for the instant swooping acceleration that would tell me Simon had been pulled down, and that we were dying. It didn't happen.

The terrible sliding stopped, and I hung silently against the slope. Three faint tugs trembled the taut rope, and I hopped up on to my leg. A wave of nausea and pain swept over me. I was glad of the freezing blasts of snow biting into my face. My head cleared as I waited for the burning to subside from my knee. Several times I had felt it twist sideways when my boot snagged, and each time the movement was unnatural. There would be a flare of agony as the knee kinked back, and parts within the joint seemed to shear past each other with a sickening gristly crunch. I had barely ceased sobbing before my boot snagged again. At the end my leg shook uncontrollably. I tried to stop it shaking, but the harder I tried, the more it shook. I pressed my face into the snow, gritted my teeth, and waited. At last it eased.

Simon had already started to climb down and the slack rope coiled past me as he descended. I looked up but failed to make out where he was. A plume of snow boiled down, hugging the slope. I could see nothing through it. If anything, the spindrift was worse than before, and that could only mean that it had begun snowing heavily. Below me the view was equally limited.

I began digging Simon's belay seat. It was warming work and distracted attention from my knee. When I looked up again Simon could be seen descending quickly.

'At this rate we should be down by nine o'clock,' he said cheerfully.

'I hope so.' I said no more. It wouldn't help to harp on about how I felt.

'Right, let's do it again.' He had seated himself in the hole and had the ropes ready for another lowering.

'You're not hanging around, are you?'

'Nothing to wait for. Come on.'

He was still grinning, and his confidence was infectious. Who said one man can't rescue another, I thought. We had changed from climbing to rescue, and the partnership had worked just as effectively. We hadn't dwelt on the accident. There had been an element of uncertainty at first, but as soon as we had started to act positively everything had come together.

'Okay, ready when you are,' I said, lying on my side again. 'Slow down a bit this time. You'll have my leg off otherwise.'

He didn't seem to hear me for I went down at an even faster pace than before, and the hammering torture began again with a vengeance. My optimism evaporated. I could think of nothing but enduring until the change-over. It came after an age, but the brief respite was too short, and before the agony had eased I was sliding down again.

I pressed my hands against the snow, vainly trying to lift my leg away from the surface. The axes dangled from their loops around my waist and my hands froze. My leg snagged. There was nothing I could do. The muscles had seized up. I tried and tried again to lift it clear of the snow, but it had fused into lumpy dead-weight. I clenched my thigh muscles in an attempt to lift it clear, but nothing happened. It was no longer a part of me. It obeyed no commands, and dangled inert and useless. It snagged, and snagged again, twisted, kinked, and caused every sort of agony, until I gave up trying and lay limp against the moving snow, sobbing. The lowering continued. I forgot about it ending, and gave myself up to the pain. It swamped round my knee and ran up my thigh, infusing all my conscious thoughts with its heat. It pitched higher with every jolt, insisting on attention, becoming something endowed with its own individuality until I could hear its message clearly – 'I'm hurt. I'm damaged. Rest me, leave me be!'

The movement stopped abruptly. Three tugs tremored down. I stood up, shaking. I tried to grab the axe to begin digging the next bucket seat but couldn't grip the shaft. When I had made it stay in my mitt, it flopped from side to side. I tried picking up the hammer, with the same result. I tugged at my right mitt but couldn't hold it tight enough to get it off and eventually ripped it free with my teeth. The blue thermal gloves stayed on my hand, ice frosted on to the fabric. Even through the gloves I could see how wooden my fingers had become. They moved stiffly and all together, and refused to curl into a fist.

Spindrift poured down the surface of the slope, filling the mitt which hung from its loop on my wrist while I held my hand under my armpit inside my jacket. The searing pain of returning blood was all I could think about. Even the mushy agony in my lower leg waned before this frightful burning heat in my fingers. When it eased, I emptied my mitt, put the gloved hand back into it, and repeated the process with the other hand.

Simon came down before I had half finished digging his belay seat. He waited silently, head bowed. When I looked at him I saw that he had both hands in his armpits.

'Mine were real bad. I thought they were frostbitten,' I said.

'It's just the lowering. They really freeze up when I'm lowering. Can't get my middle fingers to warm. They've gone altogether.'

He had his eyes tight closed, fighting the hot aches. A heavier burst of spindrift sprayed over him but he ignored it. It partially filled the seat I had been digging. I swept it clear with the side of my arm.

'Come on. It's getting bad. We'll have to hurry.'

I lay beneath his feet, and when the rope came taut I shifted my weight off my foot and tensed against the prospect of another drop. He let me down with a rush and I cried out as my boot caught in the snow. I was looking at him when I cried out. He remained expressionless, and continued to lower me. He had no time for sympathy.

By the end of the fourth drop I had deteriorated. The shaking in my leg was continuous and unstoppable. The pain had reached a level beyond which it wouldn't go. It remained constant whether I snagged my leg or not. Curiously, it had become more bearable, for I no longer winced and tensed at the prospect of catching my foot. I could adjust to the steady pain. My hands, however, were much worse. The rewarming, repeated at the end of every lowering, was less effective each time. Simon's hands were even worse than mine.

The storm had steadily increased until the spindrift flowed continually down the slope, and threatened to push me off when I dug the seats. The wind gusted across the face, blasting the snow into exposed skin, and forcing itself through the tiniest of openings in clothing. I was close to exhaustion.

As the drops continued I lapsed into resigned tolerance. The object of the lowering had long since escaped me. I couldn't think any further ahead than simply enduring the present. Simon said nothing at the change-overs, his expression fixed and rigid. We had locked ourselves into a grim struggle, my part was pain-wracked, Simon's an endless physical battle to get me down almost 3,000 feet without a break. I wondered how often it had occurred to him that the seats might collapse at any moment. I was beyond caring about such things, but Simon knew all the time that he could descend alone quite safely if he chose. I began to thank him for what he was doing, and then quickly stopped myself. It would only emphasise my dependence on him.

I dug the fifth belay seat while Simon climbed down to me. I didn't get far. After clearing the surface snow away I struck water ice. I was standing on my left foot but it wasn't kicked deeply in. I perched on the front points of my crampons, a worrying position because I could feel my calf muscles tiring from the strain, and the idea that I might slip preyed on my mind. It would rip us both off the mountain. To make matters worse, the effort of staying quite still made me feel nauseous and dizzy. I kept shaking my head and pressing it against the snow, terrified that I might faint. It seemed such a stupid way to die after we had been through so much.

It was a measure of how cold I had become to see how long it took before I thought of hammering an ice screw into the slope. The wind and constant avalanches had fogged my mind after numbing my body. Even when the idea did occur to me, it took some time to break through the lethargic apathy that engulfed me, and turning it into action seemed an achievement in itself. I was alarmed at my behaviour. I had heard of people succumbing to cold without realising it, reacting lazily and without thinking. When I had tied into the ice screw, I leant back on it and began a vigorous warming and waking exercise. I moved as much of my body as I could, flapped my arms, rubbed myself briskly and shook my head. I warmed gradually, and felt the sluggishness clear away.

Simon noticed the ice screw. It was in the only ice we had so far found on the face, and he looked at me questioningly.

'There must be something below us. A steep section, something like that,' I said.

'Yeah. I can't see a thing down there.' He was leaning out from the screw peering intently below him. 'It does get steeper but I can't see what's causing it.'

I looked down and saw only the swirling clouds of spindrift whipping down. The sky was full of snow. It was either falling, or being blown by the wind. The end result was the same – white-out conditions.

'It wouldn't be a good idea to lower me if you don't know what's below,' I said. 'It could be anything . . . a rock buttress, ice fall, anything.'

'I know, but I can't remember seeing anything very large when we were on Seria Norte. Can you?'

'No. A few rock outcrops maybe, but nothing else. Why don't you abseil down and give me some tugs if it's okay to follow. I reckon I can abseil myself.'

'We haven't any choice. Right, I'll put another screw in.'

He hammered the screw into the hard water ice and clipped the doubled rope through it. I untied from the rope, staying safely clipped into my own ice screw. When Simon reached the end of the rope he would organise a belay and then signal me to follow. I shouted to him when he had abseiled below me:

'Keep a knot in the end of the ropes. If I faint I don't want to go off the end.'

He waved acknowledgment and slid down into clouds of spindrift. He was soon lost from sight and I was alone. I tried not to think of anything happening to him. I stood quietly on one foot, gazing into the snow swirling madly round me. There was only the sound of hissing as it sprayed off my jacket, and occasional tugs from the wind. It was a wild place in which to be alone. I thought of the sun on Yerupaja through the window in the snow-cave – that was this morning! God! It seemed so very long ago. Only this morning . . . and we had come down the ridge, and over those crevasses, and then the ice cliff. A lifetime away . . . so much had changed. The cold crept through me again, and I could feel its heavy slowness spreading.

I started my warming routine again, flapping, rubbing, driving the intruder away. Then I saw the ropes jerk spasmodically. I grabbed hold of them and felt the tugs come up the ropes again. I fixed my belay plate on to the ropes, and removed the ice screw from which I had been hanging. I let my weight come down carefully on to the abseil ropes, watching the ice screw for any warning signs of failure. The ropes eased through the plate, and I slid down after Simon.

After twenty feet the slope dropped vertically under me. I stopped moving and glanced down. I could see the angle ease about fifteen feet below. Beyond there was only spindrift. As I abseiled past the wall I could see that it consisted of patches of ice plastered on to a steep rock face. It went slowly past me in short stepped walls with steep ice cascades in between. Once or twice I bumped painfully against the rock, but for the most part I found abseiling to be easier and a lot less traumatic than being lowered. I could control the speed of descent, which helped. The steep walls were entirely pain-free because I could twist away and let my injured leg hang free in space, and even on the cascades I managed to keep from snagging it.

I was concentrating on abseiling carefully, and had become quite engrossed in what I was doing, when Simon's voice broke into my thoughts. I looked down, and saw him leaning back on an ice screw grinning at me:

91

'There's one more steep bit. I saw the snow slope running below it, so it can't be far.'

As he spoke he reached out and caught hold of my waist, tugging me gently towards him. He was careful, almost tender, in the way he spun me round so that I was facing out from the slope when I came to a stop beside him. He clipped me into a second ice screw that he had placed beside the one on which he was hanging, and directed my uninjured leg to a foothold that he had hacked from the ice. I realised then that he had been fully aware of the pain he had been putting me through, and this concern was a quiet way of saying, it's all right. I wasn't being a bastard. It just had to be done.

'Not far now. Maybe another four lowers after this next abseil.'

I knew he was guessing. He was trying to cheer me up, and I felt deeply grateful. For a short moment on the storm-swept belay we had accepted a warm sense of friendship. It felt like some cliché from a third-rate war movie – We're all in this together, lads, and we're all going to make it home. It also felt true and real, something unassailable in all the uncertainty. I put my arm on his shoulder and smiled at him. Behind his grin I could see the truth of our situation. It had taken a lot out of him and he looked drawn. His face, pinched with cold, showed all the tension he had been through, and his eyes didn't smile. There was concern and anxiety there, and I could see that, despite his confident words, a dark uncertainty reflected the real story.

'I'm all right,' I said. 'The pain's not so bad now. How are your hands?'

'Bad, and getting worse.' He grinned at me, and I felt a stab of guilt. It was costing him. I had already paid.

'I'll abseil down and set up the belay.'

He stepped away from the slope and hopped smoothly into the vortex of spindrift below.

I quickly joined him at the large bucket seat he had excavated. We were back to lowering from non-existent belays. I checked my watch. I couldn't see the face, and was surprised to notice how dark it had become. When I flicked the little watch light on, I saw that it was seven thirty. It had been dark for over an hour and I hadn't noticed! It made me realise how little I had had to do. Digging belay seats and closing my mind to the lowering hadn't needed any light.

The warmth of feeling on the abseil belay stayed with me through the next drop, and I had to resist the urge to giggle excitedly as the descent continued. I felt childishly irrational. The thought of reaching the glacier and a snug snow-cave had become irresistible. It flooded through my mind like the images of a hot meal in front of the fire after a long cold day on the hills. I tried to push it away, fearful that to think this way would be to invite disaster. I want never gets, I told myself, but it didn't work. The lowering went quicker and easier. The pain stayed with me but it was secondary: getting down was all I could think about.

The system of lowering became second nature, as if we had been practising it for years, and as we slid down unseen through the storm the sense of optimism snowballed with every foot descended. Simon's grin widened at every meeting and his eyes, bright in the light from my head-torch, said it all. We had regained control of the situation, and it no longer felt as if we were fleeing in disarray or fighting desperately against the odds. We knew we were making a controlled and orderly descent.

I hunched my shoulders against an unusually heavy rush of spindrift and braced myself until it spent itself. Moving again, the build-up of snow between my chest and the slope flowed down over my legs, and I brushed the powder from the belay seat I had dug. The weather showed no sign of improving, but at least it was not getting worse. Simon appeared from the murk above me. His light flashed yellow off the clouds of snow. I kept looking at him so that my head-torch light would guide him down. He reached me as another avalanche swept over us. We both ducked.

'Bloody hell! That one before nearly knocked me off.'

'They've been getting bigger. Probably because we're near the bottom. There's more snow to build up on the way down.'

'I was thinking of unroping. Then I won't take you down if

I get hit hard.' I laughed. If he fell past me, leaving me the rope, I would be able to do nothing with it.

'I'd fall anyway, so you might as well stay roped. That way I won't have to think about it . . . and I can blame you!'

He didn't laugh. He had almost forgotten that I was hurt, and now I had reminded him. He settled himself into the seat and arranged the ropes for the next lowering.

'Two lowers to go at the most, I reckon. This will be the eighth, plus the two abseils, so we've covered two thousand seven hundred feet, or thereabouts. It can't be more than three thousand, so this might even be the last one.'

I nodded in agreement, and he grinned confidently at me as I slid down the slope and he faded into the snowstorm. Earlier, I had noticed that the angle of the slope was gradually easing. I took this as an encouraging sign which indicated how close we were getting to the glacier. However, soon after I lost sight of Simon I noticed the slope steepening again. I slid faster, and snagged my foot more frequently. I was distracted by the pain and discomfort, and thought no more of the slope. I struggled vainly to clear my foot from the snow before giving up and accepting the torment.

The sense of weight on my harness increased, as did the speed. I tried braking with my arms but to no effect. I twisted round and looked up into the darkness. Rushes of snow flickered in my torch beam. I yelled for Simon to slow down. The speed increased, and my heart jumped wildly. Had he lost control? I tried braking again. Nothing. I stifled the rising panic and tried to think clearly – no, he hadn't lost control. I'm going down fast but it's steady. He's trying to be quick . . . that's all. I knew it to be true, but there was still something wrong.

It was the slope. Of course! I should have thought of it earlier. It was now much steeper, and that could mean only one thing – I was approaching another drop.

I screamed out a frantic warning but he couldn't hear me. I shouted again, as loud as I could, but the words were whipped away into the snow clouds. He wouldn't have heard me fifteen feet away. I tried to guess how far I was from the half-way knot. A hundred feet? Fifty? I had no idea. Each lowering became timeless. I slid for ever through the boiling snow without any sense of time passing – just a barely endurable period of agony.

A sense of great danger washed over me. I *had* to stop. I realised that Simon would hear nothing, so I must stop myself. If he felt my weight come off the rope he would know there must be a good reason. I grabbed my ice axe and tried to brake my descent. I leant heavily over the axe head, burying it in the slope, but it wouldn't bite. The snow was too loose. I dug my left boot into the slope but it, too, just scraped through the snow.

Then abruptly my feet were in space. I had time to cry out, and claw hopelessly at the snow before my whole body swung off an edge. I jerked on to the rope and toppled over backwards, spinning in circles from my harness. The rope ran up to a lip of ice and I saw that I was still descending. The sight vanished as a heavy avalanche of powder poured over me.

When it ceased I realised that I had stopped moving. Simon had managed to hold the impact of my body suddenly coming on to the rope. I was confused. I didn't understand what had happened, except that I was hanging free in space. I grabbed the rope and pulled myself up into a sitting position. The spinning continued but it was slowing down. I could see an ice wall six feet away from me every time I completed a spin. When I stopped spinning I was facing away from the wall and had to twist round to look at it. The spindrift had stopped. I shone my torch up the wall following the line of the rope until I could make out the edge I had gone over. It was about fifteen feet above me. The wall was solid ice and steeply overhanging. The rope jerked down a few inches, then stopped. Another avalanche of powder poured over the edge, and the wind blew it in eddies round me. I hunched protectively.

Looking between my legs, I could see the wall dropping below, angled away from me. It was overhanging all the way to the bottom. I stared down trying to judge the height of the wall. I thought I could see the snow-covered base of the wall with the dark outline of a crevasse directly beneath me, then snow flurries blocked my view. I looked back at the edge above. There was no chance of Simon hauling me up. It would have been extremely hard with a solid belay. Sitting in the snow seat, it would be suicidal to attempt it. I shouted at the darkness above and heard an unintelligible muffled yell. I couldn't be sure whether it had been Simon or an echo of my own shout.

I waited silently, hugging the rope with my arms to stay upright, and feeling shocked as I stared between my legs at the drop. Gradually, and with a sense of mounting dread, I began to get some perspective into what I was looking at. I was an awfully long way above the crevasse at the base of the cliff, and as it slowly dawned on me I felt my stomach lurch with fear. There was at least 100 feet of air below my feet! I kept staring at the drop, hoping to find I was mistaken. I realised that, far from being wrong, I had been conservative in my estimate. For a moment I did nothing while my thoughts whirled and I tried to assess how things had changed. Then one fact jolted through my thoughts.

I swung round and stared at the wall. It was six feet from me. At full arm's reach, I still couldn't reach the ice with my axe. I tried swinging towards the wall but ended up spinning helplessly. I knew that I had to get back up the rope, and I had to do it quickly: Simon had no idea what I'd gone over. The other steep drops were short walls. He had no reason to assume this would be any different. In that case he might lower me. Oh, Jesus, I'll jam on the half-way knot long before I get to the bottom!

It was impossible to reach the wall, and I realised quickly that it wouldn't help me. I couldn't climb fifteen feet of overhanging ice with one leg. I fumbled at my waist for the two loops of rope I had tied there. I found them but couldn't grip them with my mitts on. I wrenched off the mitts with my teeth and reached for the two loops again. I slipped one over my wrist and held the second in my teeth. In reaching for the loops I had let go of the rope and tumbled over backwards so that I hung from the waist. My rucksack had pulled me over, and I hung in an inverted curve with my head and legs lower than my waist. I struggled to swing up until I reached the rope and pulled myself back to a sitting position.

I crooked my left arm around the rope to hold me upright, and took the loop from my teeth with my right hand. I tried to twist the thin loop of cord around the rope but my fingers were too numbed. I needed to get a Prussik knot on to the rope, so that I could slide the knot up and hang in tension as the knot tightened. The effort of holding myself up was exhausting. At last, using a combination of teeth and hand, I managed to twist the loop around the rope, and then tried repeating the process. I needed at least three twists before the knot would be of any use. By the time I had succeeded I was almost crying with frustration. It had taken me nearly fifteen minutes. The wind nudged me into a gentle spin and blasted the incessant avalanches into my face, blinding me. I clipped a karabiner into the Prussik loop and fastened it to my waist.

I shoved the loop as far up the rope as I could reach and leant back on it. The knot tightened, slipped a few inches, and then held me. I let go of the rope and hung back. I remained sitting up. The second loop had to be tied on to the rope but this time I would be able to use both hands.

It wasn't until I tried to slip it off my left wrist that I realised how useless my hands were. Both were frozen. I could move the fingers of my right hand, but my left hand, which had been still as I held on to the rope, had seized. I thumped them together, bending the fingers in against my palms. I hit them, bent them, hit them, again and again, but there were no hot aches. Some movement and feeling returned but it was minimal.

I took the loop from my wrist and held it against the rope. At my first attempt to twist it around and back inside itself I dropped it. It fell on to the main rope knot on my harness and I grabbed at it before it was blown off. Then, as I lifted it to the rope, it seemed to slide out of my hand. I grabbed at it with my left hand and managed to catch it against my right forearm. I couldn't pick it up. My fingers refused to close round it, and as I tried slipping it up my arm it dropped again. This time I watched it fall away beneath me. I knew at once that I now had no chance of climbing up the rope. It would have been hard enough doing it with two loops, and now, with both hands so useless, I had no chance. I slumped on to the rope and swore bitterly.

At least I wasn't having to hold myself up. It was a consolation although I knew it achieved little else. The rope ran up from my waist taut as an iron bar. The loop I had attached gripped the rope three feet above my harness. I unclipped it from my harness and then threaded it through my rucksack straps so that it pulled them together across my chest. I fastened it with my last karabiner and leant back to test it. The effect was good. The loop now held my torso up on the rope so that I sat in space as if in an armchair. When I was sure it was as good as I could get it, I slumped back on to the rope feeling utterly weary.

The wind gusted against me, making me swing crazily on the rope, and with each gust I was getting colder. The pressure of the harness on my waist and thighs had cut off the circulation and both legs felt numb. The pain in the knee had gone. I let my arms hang slackly, feeling the deadweight of useless hands in my mitts. There was no point in reviving them. There was no way out of this slow hanging. I couldn't go up, and Simon would never get me down. I tried to work out how long it had been since I had gone over the edge. I decided it could be no more than half an hour. In two hours I would be dead. I could feel the cold taking me.

Twinges of fear lurked round my mind but even these were fading as it crept through me. I was interested in the sensations, wondering idly how it would take me. At least it wouldn't hurt – I was glad of that; the hurting had worn me out and it felt so calm now that it was over. Above my waist the cold slowed its progress. I fancied how it would ease its way up, following veins and arteries, creeping inexorably through me. I thought of it as something living; something which lived through crawling into my body. I knew it didn't work like that, but it felt as if it did, and that seemed a good enough reason to believe it. I wasn't going to argue about it with anyone; of that I could be sure. I almost laughed out loud at the idea. I felt so tired; sleepy tired, and weak. I had never felt so weak; a limbless, disembodied feeling. It was odd.

I jerked down sharply, and bounced on the rope. When I turned to look at the wall I realised I was going down. Simon was lowering me again. I shook my head, trying to clear the lethargy. He had no chance. I was sure that he was gambling on being able to get me down before the knot jammed. Secretly I hoped he could, and knew with certainty that he had no chance. I screamed a warning into the night. There was no reply. I continued falling steadily. I looked down and saw the crevasse below me. I could see it clearly. When I looked up I could no longer make out the top of the cliff. The ropes ran up into snow flurries and disappeared. There was a small jerk, then another, and I stopped.

Half an hour passed. I stopped shouting at Simon. I knew he was in the same situation as me, unable to move. Either he would die in his seat or be pulled from it by the constant strain of my body. I wondered whether I would die before this happened. It would happen as soon as he lost consciousness, and maybe he would do so before me. On the rope I was clear of the worst avalanches. He would be colder than me.

Each thought of death, of mine or his, came quite unemotionally – matter-of-fact. I was too tired to care. Perhaps if I was scared I would fight harder, I thought, and then dismissed the idea. I was scared tying the loops and it hadn't helped. Toni Kurtz had fought and fought when he was dying on the Eiger. He had never once stopped fighting, and he had dropped suddenly dead on the rope still fighting to live. Rescuers had watched him die. It seemed strange to be in the same situation and not be bothered . . . maybe it's the cold? Won't be long now. I'll not last till morning . . . won't see the sun either. I hope Simon doesn't die, that's hard . . . he shouldn't have to die for me . . .

I jerked upright, the drifting aimless thoughts pushed away and replaced with a consuming anger at what had happened. I screamed at the wind. Swearing and yelling blind.

'On the last bloody lower, and after all that pain. YOU SHIT. YOU FUCKING BASTARD.'

Words wasted into the snow and wind, shouted to no one in particular in a shaking fury of bitterness and grievance. Idiot words, as meaningless as the hissing empty wind around me. Anger surged through me. It warmed me, shook me, driving the cold off in a tirade of obscenities and frustrated tears. I cried for myself and swore at myself. Everything came down to me. It was *my* knee that was smashed. *I* had fallen, and *I* was dying, and Simon with me.

The rope slipped. I bounced down a few inches. Then again. Had he freed the knot? I slipped again. Stopped. Then I knew what was about to happen. He was coming down. I was pulling him off. I hung still, and waited for it to happen. Any minute, any minute . . .

Joe had smiled as I let him slide away from me. It wasn't much of a smile. His pain twisted it into a grimace. I let him go fast and ignored his cries. He was quickly gone from my torch beam, and as another avalanche swept over my head the rope disappeared as well. Apart from his weight on my waist there was no sign of his existence.

I kept the speed going. The belay plate was easy to control despite my deadened fingers. They were bad now. I worried about them, as I had done since we left the col. I knew Joe's climbing days were over, but now I was scared for my hands. There was no telling how bad they would be. I had a quick look when it was light but I couldn't see how deep the damage was. Four fingertips were blackened, and one thumb, but there was no saying whether the others wouldn't also go the same way.

I heard a faint cry from below, and the rope jerked slightly. Poor bastard, I thought. I had hurt him all the way down. It was strange being so cold about it. It had been hard not to feel for him. It was easier now. We had made such fast progress. Efficient. I felt proud about it. We had held it all together, and that was good. The lowering had been easier than I had expected, especially with Joe digging the seats for me. He had really held it together. That was some control! I'd never asked him to dig the seats, but he just went ahead and did it. Wonder whether I would have done that? Who knows.

My hands were stiffening again. They always got bad before the knot; stiff, like claws. The rope ran out smoothly. I had been careful to avoid any tangles. The idea of holding Joe with one hand and trying to unsnarl a tangled and frozen rope didn't bear thinking about. The pull at my harness increased. The slope must be steepening again, I thought. There were another seventy feet to go before the half-way knot had to be changed over. I increased the rate of descent. I knew it was hurting him. When it had been light I could see his pain for a long way down, but we had got down. It was necessary. Another faint cry came from the darkness. A rushing flow of snow poured over me again. I hunched deeper into the seat, feeling the snow settle and crumble slightly. The seats lasted for the lower but by then they were well on their way to collapse.

Suddenly I jolted heavily forward from the waist and nearly came out of the seat. I threw my weight back and down into the snow, bracing my legs hard against the sudden pressure. Christ! Joe's fallen. I let the rope slide slowly to a stop trying to avoid the impact I would have got if I had stopped it dead. The pressure remained constant. My harness bit into my hips, and the rope pulling tautly between my legs threatened to rip me down through the floor of the seat.

After half an hour I let the rope slide again. Whatever Joe had gone over had stopped him getting his weight off the rope. My legs had numbed as the pressure on my hips cut the blood supply away. I tried to think of something to do other than lower. There was nothing. Joe had not attempted to climb back up. I had felt no trembling in the rope to tell me he was attempting something. There was no chance of hauling him up. Already the seat was half its original size. It had steadily disintegrated from beneath my thighs. I couldn't hold the weight much longer. The steep sections higher on the face had been less than fifty feet high. I decided that he would be able to get his weight off the rope after a short distance, and set a belay up. I had no choice.

As the rope ran out I realised that the pressure wasn't easing. Joe was still hanging free. What in hell's name was I lowering him over?

I looked down at the slack rope being fed through the belay plate. Twenty feet below I spotted the knot coming steadily towards me. I began swearing, trying to urge Joe to touch down on to something solid. At ten feet I stopped lowering. The pressure on the rope hadn't changed.

I kept stamping my feet. I was trying to halt the collapse of the seat but it wasn't working. I felt the first shivers of fear. Snow hit me again from behind, surging over and around me. My thighs moved down fractionally. The avalanche pushed me forward and filled the seat behind my back. Oh God! I'm coming off.

Then it stopped as abruptly as it had started. I let the rope slide five feet, thinking furiously. Could I hold the rope with one hand below the knot and change the plate over? I lifted one hand from the rope and stared at it. I couldn't squeeze it into a fist. I thought of holding the rope locked against the plate by winding it round my thigh and then releasing the plate from my harness. Stupid idea! I couldn't hold Joe's weight with my hands alone. If I released the plate, 150 feet of free rope would run unstoppable through my hands, and then it would rip me clear off the mountain.

It had been nearly an hour since Joe had gone over the drop. I was shaking with cold. My grip on the rope kept easing despite my efforts. The rope slowly edged down and the knot pressed against my right fist. I can't hold it, can't stop it. The thought overwhelmed me. The snow slides and wind and cold were forgotten. I was being pulled off. The seat moved beneath me, and snow slipped away past my feet. I slipped a few inches. Stamping my feet deep into the slope halted the movement. God! I had to do something!

The knife! The thought came out of nowhere. Of course, the knife. Be quick, come on, get it.

The knife was in my sack. It took an age to let go a hand and slip the strap off my shoulder, and then repeat it with the other hand. I braced the rope across my thigh and held on to *the plate with my right hand as hard as I could. Fumbling at the catches on the rucksack, I could feel the snow slowly giving way beneath me. Panic threatened to swamp me. I felt in the sack, searching desperately for the knife. My hand closed round something smooth and I pulled it out. The red plastic handle slipped in my mitt and I nearly dropped it. I put it in my lap before tugging my mitt off with my teeth. I had already made the decision. There was no other option left to me. The metal blade stuck to my lips when I opened it with my teeth.*

I reached down to the rope and then stopped. The slack rope! Clear the loose rope twisted round my foot! If it tangled it would rip me down with it. I carefully cleared it to one side, and checked that it all lay in the seat away from the belay plate. I reached down again, and this time I touched the blade to the rope.

It needed no pressure. The taut rope exploded at the touch of the blade, and I flew backwards into the seat as the pulling strain vanished. I was shaking.

Leaning back against the snow, I listened to a furious hammering in my temple as I tried to calm my breathing. Snow hissed over me in a torrent. I ignored it as it poured over my face and chest, spurting into the open zip at my neck, and on down below. It kept coming. Washing across me and down after the cut rope, and after Joe.

I was alive, and for the moment that was all I could think about. Where Joe was, or whether he was alive, didn't concern me in the long silence after the cutting. His weight had gone from me. There was only the wind and the avalanches left to me.

When at last I sat up, the slack rope fell from my hips. One frayed end protruded from the belay plate – he had gone. Had I killed him? – I didn't answer the thought, though some urging in the back of my mind told me that I had. I felt numb. Freezing cold, and shocked into a numb silence, I stared bleakly into the swirling snow beneath me wondering at what had happened. There was no guilt, not even sorrow. I stared at the faint torch beam cutting through the snow and felt haunted by its emptiness. I was tempted to shout to him, but stifled the cry. It wouldn't be heard. I could be sure of that. I shivered in the wind as the cold crept up my back. Another avalanche swept over me in the darkness. Alone on a storm-swept avalanching mountain face, and becoming dangerously cold, I was left with no choice but to forget about Joe until the morning.

I stood up and turned into the slope. The belay seat was full of avalanched powder. I started to dig and soon I had excavated a sufficiently large hole to lie half-buried in the slope with only my legs exposed to the storm. I dug automatically while my mind wandered through tortured arguments and asked unanswerable questions, and then I stopped digging and lay still, thinking about the night. Then I dug again. Every few minutes I would shake myself from a mess of thoughts and return to digging, only to find I had drifted off again a few minutes later. It took a long time to complete the cave.

It was a weird night. It felt strange to think so coldly about what had happened, as if I were distancing myself from the events. Occasionally I wondered whether Joe was still alive. I had no idea what he had fallen over. I knew how close we had come to the bottom of the mountain, so it seemed reasonable to hope that he might survive a short fall to the glacier, could even now be digging a snow cave himself. Something made me think this wasn't the case, and I couldn't evade the urgent feeling that he must be dead or dying. I sensed that something awful was hidden in the powder avalanches swirling madly through the black night below my snow cave.

When the cave was finished I struggled into my sleeping bag and blocked the entrance with my rucksack. The wind and the avalanches rushing across the roof could not be heard, and I lay in the silent darkness trying to sleep. Plagued with endless thoughts which turned madly upon themselves in vicious circles, sleep was impossible. I tried to get my mind to settle by looking back on what I had done and thinking it all through. After a while I stopped, having succeeded only in recalling the facts, and they were so starkly real that I could draw no conclusions from them. I wanted to question what I had done. It seemed necessary to prosecute myself, and to prove that I had been wrong.

The result was worse than the vicious circles which had made me think it through. I argued that I was satisfied with myself. I was actually pleased that I had been strong enough to cut the rope. There had been nothing else left to me, and so I had gone ahead with it. I had done it, and done it well. Shit! That takes some doing! A lot of people would have died before getting it together to do that! I was still alive because I had held everything together right up to the last moment. It had been executed calmly. I had even carefully stopped to check that the rope wasn't going to tangle and pull me down. So that's why I feel so damned confused! I should feel guilty. I don't. I did right. But, what of Joe . . .

Eventually I dozed and spent a few troubled hours lost in sleep between waking hours of thinking. Thinking blind in a dark, storm-swept cave. Thinking because my mind refused to sleep, or because I was so pumped-up on strain and fear and dread. Thinking, Joe's dead, I know he's dead, in a monotonous litany, and then not thinking of him as Joe any more, only the weight gone off from my waist so suddenly and violently that I couldn't fully grasp it all.

As the night lengthened I sank into a dazed confusion, and Joe faded from memory. It was thirst that took his place, and with each awakening I craved water until it governed my every thought. My tongue felt dry and swollen. It stuck to my palate, and no amount of snow crammed into my mouth could kill the thirst. It was nearly twenty-four hours since I had taken a drink. In that time I should have had at least one and a half litres of fluid to make up for the dehydration caused by the altitude. I smelt the water in the snow around me and it maddened me. I dozed into exhausted stupors, only to wake abruptly to an insistent craving for liquid.

It gradually lightened. I saw axe marks on the roof, and the night was over. With the coming of day I thought of what I must do. I knew I wouldn't succeed. It wasn't right for me to succeed. I had thought it all through. This was what must *happen to me now. I was no longer afraid, and the dread in the night had gone with the dawn. I knew I would attempt it, and I knew it would kill me, but I was going to go through with it. There would be some dignity left to me at least. I had to try my best. It wouldn't be enough, but I would try.*

I dressed like a priest before mass, with solemn careful ceremony. I felt in no hurry to start down and was certain it would be my last day. Filled with a sense of condemnation, I prepared for the day in such a way that it felt as if I were part of an ancient universal ritual, a long-planned ritual which had been born during the dark thought-wracked hours behind me.

I fastened the last strap of my crampons on to my boot, and then stared silently at my gloved hands. The careful preparation had calmed me. My fear had gone and I was quiet. I felt cold and hard. The night had cleaned me out, purging the guilt and the pain. The loneliness since the cutting had also gone. The thirst had eased. I was as ready as I would ever be.

I smashed the roof of the cave with my axe, and stood up into the blinding glare of a perfect day. No avalanches, and no wind. Silent ice mountains gleamed white around me, and the glacier curved gently westwards to the black moraines above base camp. I felt watched. Something in the crescent of summits and ridges looked down on me and waited. I stepped from the wreckage of the cave, and started to climb down. I was about to die; I knew it, and they knew it.

7

Shadows in the Ice

I lolled on the rope, scarcely able to hold my head up. An awful weariness washed through me, and with it a fervent hope that this endless hanging would soon be over. There was no need for the torture. I wanted with all my heart for it to finish.

The rope jolted down a few inches. How long will you be, Simon? I thought. How long before you join me? It would be soon. I could feel the rope tremble again; wire-tight, it told me the truth as well as any phone call. So! It ends here. Pity! I hope somebody finds us, and knows we climbed the West Face. I don't want to disappear without trace. They'd never know we did it.

The wind swung me in a gentle circle. I looked at the crevasse beneath me, waiting for me. It was big. Twenty feet wide at least. I guessed that I was hanging fifty feet above it. It stretched along the base of the ice cliff. Below me it was covered with a roof of snow, but to the right it opened out and a dark space yawned there. Bottomless, I thought idly. No. They're never bottomless. I wonder how deep I will go? To the bottom . . . to the water at the bottom? God! I hope not!

Another jerk. Above me the rope sawed through the cliff edge, dislodging chunks of crusty ice. I stared at it stretching into the darkness above. Cold had long since won its battle. There was no feeling in my arms and legs. Everything slowed and softened. Thoughts became idle questions, never answered. I accepted that I was to die. There was no alternative. It caused me no dreadful fear. I was numb with cold and felt no pain; so senselessly cold that I craved sleep and cared nothing for the consequences. It would be a dreamless sleep. Reality had become a nightmare, and sleep beckoned insistently; a black hole calling me, pain-free, lost in time, like death.

My torch beam died. The cold had killed the batteries. I saw stars in a dark gap above me. Stars, or lights in my head. The storm was over. The stars were good to see. I was glad to see them again. Old friends come back. They seemed far away; further than I'd ever seen them before. And bright: you'd think them gemstones hanging there, floating in the air above. Some moved, little winking moves, on and off, on and off, floating the brightest sparks of light down to me.

Then, what I had waited for pounced on me. The stars went out, and I fell. Like something come alive, the rope lashed violently against my face and I fell silently, endlessly into nothingness, as if dreaming of falling. I fell fast, faster than thought, and my stomach protested at the swooping speed of it. I swept down, and from far above I saw myself falling and felt nothing. No thoughts, and all fears gone away. So this is it!

A whoomphing impact on my back broke the dream, and the snow engulfed me. I felt cold wetness on my cheeks. I wasn't stopping, and for an instant blinding moment I was frightened. Now, the crevasse! Ahhh . . . NO!!

The acceleration took me again, mercifully fast, too fast for the scream which died above me . . .

The whitest flashes burst in my eyes as a terrible impact whipped me into stillness. The flashes continued, bursting electric flashes in my eyes as I heard, but never felt, the air rush from my body. Snow followed down on to me, and I registered its soft blows from far away, hearing it scrape over me in a distant disembodied way. Something in my head seemed to pulse and fade, and the flashes came less frequently. The shock had stunned me so that for an immeasurable time I lay numb, hardly conscious of what had happened. As in dreams, time had slowed, and I seemed motionless in the air, unsupported, without mass. I lay still, with open mouth, open eyes staring into blackness, thinking they were closed, and noting every sensation, all the pulsing messages in my body, and did nothing.

I couldn't breathe. I retched. Nothing. Pressure pain in my chest. Retching, and gagging, trying hard for the air. Nothing. I felt a familiar dull roaring sound of shingles on a beach, and relaxed. I shut my eyes, and gave in to grey fading shadows. My chest spasmed, then heaved out, and the roaring in my head suddenly cleared as cold air flowed in.

I was alive.

A burning, searing agony reached up from my leg. It was bent beneath me. As the burning increased so the sense of living became fact. Heck! I couldn't be dead and feel that! It kept burning, and I laughed – Alive! Well, fuck me! – and laughed again, a real happy laugh. I laughed through the burning, and kept laughing hard, feeling tears rolling down my face. I couldn't see what was so damned funny, but I laughed anyway. Crying and laughing at high pitch as something uncurled within me, something tight and twisted in my guts that laughed itself apart and left me.

I stopped laughing abruptly. My chest tightened, and the tension took hold again.

What stopped me?

I could see nothing. I lay on my side, crumpled strangely. I moved an arm cautiously in an arc. I touched a hard wall. Ice! It was the wall of the crevasse. I continued the search, and suddenly felt my arm drop into space. There was a drop close by me. I stifled the urge to move away from it. Behind me I felt my legs lying against a slope of snow. It also sloped steeply beneath me. I was on a ledge, or a bridge. I wasn't slipping, but I didn't know which way to move to make myself safe. Face down in the snow I tried to gather my confused ideas into a plan. What should I do now?

Just keep still. That's it . . . *don't move* . . . Ah!

I couldn't stop myself. Pain in my knee jolted through me, demanding movement. I had to get my weight off it. I moved, and slipped. Every muscle gripped down at the snow – *DON'T MOVE.*

The movement slowed, then stopped. I gasped, having held

my breath for too long. Reaching out again I felt my hand touch the hard ice wall. Then I groped for the ice hammer attached to a lanyard of thin cord clipped to my harness. Fumbling in the dark, I found the cord running tightly away from me and pulled it, bringing the hammer up out of the drop in front of me. I had to hammer an ice screw into the wall without pushing myself off the ledge I was perched on.

It proved harder than I expected. Once I had found the last remaining screw attached to my harness I had to twist round and face the wall. My eyes had adjusted to the darkness. Starlight and the moon glimmering through my entry hole in the roof above gave enough light for me to see the abysses on either side of me. I could see grey-shadowed ice walls and the stark blackness of the drops, too deep for the light to penetrate. As I began to hammer the screw into the ice I tried to ignore the black space beyond my shoulder. The hammer blows echoed around the ice walls, and from deep below me, from the depths of blackness at my shoulder, I heard second and third echoes drift up. I shuddered. The black space held untold horrors. I hit the screw, and felt my body slide sideways with each blow. When it was driven in to its hilt I clipped a karabiner through the eye and hurriedly searched for the rope at my waist. The black spaces menaced and my stomach knotted in empty squeezing clenches.

I hauled myself into a half-sitting position close to the wall, facing the drop on my left. My legs kept slipping on the snow so that I had constantly to shuffle back to the wall. I dared not let go of the ice screw for more than a few seconds, but my fingers needed a lot longer to tie the knot. I swore bitterly each time I made a mess of the knot and feverishly tried again. I couldn't see the rope, and although normally I could tie the knot blindfold, I was now hampered by frozen hands. I couldn't feel the rope well enough to thread it back on itself and form the knot. After six attempts I was at the point of tears. I dropped the rope. Reaching for it I slipped forward towards the drop and lunged back scrabbling at the wall for the screw. My mitt slipped across the wall, and I began to fall backwards. I clawed at the ice trying to get my fingers to grip through the mitts, and then felt the screw hit my hand. My fingers locked round it, and the fall stopped. I stayed motionless, staring at the black hole in front of me.

After several abortive attempts suddenly I found that I had tied a knot of sorts. I held it close to my face and looked up through it at the dim light shining through the entry hole in the roof above. I could see the bulge of the knot, and above it the loop I had been struggling to tie. I chuckled excitedly, feeling ridiculously pleased with myself, and clipped it to the ice screw, smiling foolishly into the darkness. I was safe from the black spaces.

I relaxed against the comforting tightness of the rope and looked up at the small hole in the roof, where the sky was cloudless, packed with stars, and moonlight was adding its glow to their bright sparkle. The screwed-up tension in my stomach flowed away, and for the first time in many hours I began to order my mind into normal thoughts. I'm only, what . . . fifty feet down this crevasse. It's sheltered. I can get out in the morning if I wait for Simon . . .

'SIMON!?'

I spoke his name aloud in a startled voice. The word echoed softly back. It hadn't occurred to me that he might be dead, and as I thought about what had happened the enormity of it struck me. Dead? I couldn't conceive of him dead, *not now, not after I've survived*. The chill silence of the crevasse came over me; the feel of tombs, of space for the lifeless, coldly impersonal. No one had ever been here. Simon, dead? Can't be! I'd have heard him, seen him come over the cliff. He would have come on to the rope, or down here.

I began to giggle again. Despite my efforts I couldn't prevent it, and the echoes bounced back at me from the ice walls, sounding cracked and manic. It became so that I couldn't work out whether I was laughing or sobbing. The noises that returned from the darkness were distorted and inhuman, cackling echoes rolling up and around me. I giggled more, listened and giggled again, and for a moment forgot Simon, and the crevasse, and even my leg. I sat, hunched against the ice wall, laughing convulsively, and shivering. It

111

was the cold. Part of me recognised this; a calm rational voice in my head told me it was the cold and the shock. The rest of me went quietly mad while this calm voice told me what was happening and left me feeling as if I were split in two – one half laughing, and the other looking on with unemotional objectivity. After a time I realised it had all stopped, and I was whole again. I had shivered some warmth back, and the adrenalin from the fall had gone.

I searched in my rucksack for the spare torch battery I knew was there. When I had fitted it, I switched on the beam and looked into the black space by my side. The bright new beam cut down through the blackness and lit ice walls that danced away down into depths my torch couldn't reach. The ice caught the light, so that it gleamed in blue, silver and green reflections, and I could see small rocks frozen into the surface dotted the walls at regular intervals. They glistened wetly as I swept the beam down the smooth scalloped dimples. I swallowed nervously. By the light I could see down into 100 feet of space. The walls, twenty feet apart, showed no sign of narrowing. I could only guess at how many hundreds of feet the blackness beyond my torch was hiding. In front of me the opposite wall of the crevasse reared up in a tangle of broken ice blocks and fifty feet above me they arched over to form a roof. The slope to my right fell away steeply for about thirty feet, after which it disappeared. Beyond it lay a drop into darkness.

The darkness beyond the light gripped my attention. I could guess what it hid, and I was filled with dread. I felt trapped, and looked quickly around me for some break in the walls. There was none. Ice flashed light back from hard blank walls, or else the beam was swallowed by the impenetrable blackness of the holes on either side. The roof covered the crevasse to my right and fell down in frozen chaos to my left, blocking the open end of the crevasse from my view. I was in a huge cavern of snow and ice. Only the small black hole above, winking starlights at me, gave any view of another world, and unless I climbed the blocks it was as unreachable as the stars.

I turned the torch off to save the batteries. The darkness seemed more oppressive than ever. Discovering what I had fallen into hadn't cleared my mind. I was alone. The silent emptiness, and the dark, and the star-filled hole above, mocked my thoughts of escape. I could only think of Simon. He was the only chance of escape, but somehow I was convinced that if he was not dead, then he would think that I was. I shouted his name as loud as I could, and the sound jumped back at me, and then faded in dying echoes in the holes below me. The sound would never be heard through the walls of snow and ice. The roof was fifty feet above me. On the rope I had hung at least fifty feet above the roof. Simon would see the huge open side of the crevasse, and the cliff, and he would know at once that I was dead. You can't fall that far and survive. That's what he would think. I knew it. I would think the same if I were in his place. He would see the endless black hole and know that I had died in it. The irony of falling 100 feet and surviving unscathed was almost unbearable.

I swore bitterly, and the echoes from the darkness made it a futile gesture. I swore again, and kept swearing, filling the chamber with angry obscenities which cursed me back in echoes. I screamed frustration and anger until my throat dried, and I could shout no more. When I was silent I tried to think of what would happen. If he looks in he will see me. He might even hear me. Maybe he heard me just then? He won't leave unless he's sure. How do you know he's not dead already? Did he fall with me? Find out . . . pull the rope!

I tugged on the loose rope. It moved easily. When I turned my torch on I noticed it hanging down from the hole in the roof. It hung in a slack curve. I pulled again and soft snow flurried on to me. I pulled steadily, and as I did so I became excited. This was a chance to escape. I waited for the rope to come tight. I wanted it to come tight. It kept moving easily. It was strange to want the weight of Simon's body to come on to the rope. I had instantly found a way to get out, and it meant only that. When Simon had fallen he would have swept out and clear of the crevasse. So he must have hit the slope and stopped. He would be dead. He must be after that fall.

When the rope comes tight I can Prussik up it. His body will anchor it solidly. Yes. That's it . . .

I saw the rope flick down, and my hopes sank. I drew the slack rope to me, and stared at the frayed end. Cut! I couldn't take my eyes from it. White and pink nylon filaments sprayed out from the end. I suppose I had known all along. It was a madness. Crazy to have believed in it, but everything was getting that way. I wasn't meant to get out of here. Damn it! I shouldn't even have got this far. He should have left me on the ridge. It would have saved so much . . . I'll die here after all that. Why bother trying?

I turned off the torch and sobbed quietly in the dark, feeling overwhelmed. I cried in bursts, and between them listened to the childlike sounds fade beneath me, then cried again.

It was cold when I awoke. I came up slowly from a long emptiness and wondered where I was. Sleep had taken me unawares, and I was startled. The cold had woken me. That was a good sign. It could as easily have taken me. I felt calm. It was going to end in the crevasse. Perhaps I had always known it would end this way. I felt pleased to be able to accept it calmly. All that sobbing and shouting had been too much. Acceptance seemed better. There was no trauma this way. I was certain then that Simon would leave me for dead. It didn't surprise me. Indeed it made things easier. There was one less thing to worry about. I thought it might take me a few days to die. In the end I decided that three days would pass. It was sheltered in the crevasse, and with my sleeping bag I could survive a good few days. I imagined how long it would seem; a long long period of twilight, and darkness, drifting from exhausted sleep into half-consciousness. Maybe the last half would be dreamless sleeping, ebbing away quietly. I thought carefully of the end. It wasn't how I had ever imagined it. It seemed pretty sordid. I hadn't expected a blaze of glory when it came, nor had I thought it would be like this slow pathetic fade into nothing. I didn't want it to be like that.

I sat up and turned on the torch. Looking at the wall above the ice screw, I thought it might be possible to climb out. Deep inside I knew it would be impossible, but I urged the faint hope on, deciding that if I fell then at least it would be swift. My resolve failed me when I looked at the black void on either side of me. The ice bridge suddenly seemed to be desperately precarious. I fastened a Prussik knot to the rope above the screw. I would climb while still attached to the screw. I could let slack rope out through the Prussik but if I fell the Prussik might stop me. I knew it would probably snap but I couldn't summon enough nerve to climb unroped.

An hour later I gave up trying. I had made four attempts to climb the vertical ice wall. Only once had I managed to get myself clear of the ledge. I had planted both axes above me, and hauled myself up. When I had kicked the crampons on my left boot into the wall, I reached up again with an axe. Before I could swing at the ice above, my crampon points broke free, and I slipped heavily on to my ice hammer. It ripped from the ice, and I fell back to the bridge, my injured leg folding agonisingly beneath me. I screamed, and twisted to free it. Then I lay still, waiting for the pain to ease. I would not try again.

I sat on my sack, turned off the torch, and slumped on to the rope which I had retied to the ice screw. I could see my legs in the gloom. There was a delay before I realised the significance of being able to see them. I glanced up to the patch of dim light in the roof and checked my watch. It was five o'clock. It would be fully light in an hour, and Simon would be coming down the cliff as soon as it was light. I had been alone in the dark for seven hours, and until then I hadn't realised how demoralising the lack of light had been. I shouted Simon's name, loudly. It echoed round me, and I shouted again. I would shout regularly until he heard me, or until I was certain he had gone.

A long time later I stopped shouting. He had gone. I knew he would, and I knew he wouldn't return. I was dead. There would be nothing for him to come back for. I took my mitts and inner gloves off, and examined my fingers. Two blackened fingers on each hand, and one bluish thumb. I curled them into fists and tried to squeeze hard but couldn't feel the pressure. It wasn't as bad as I had thought. Sunlight

115

streamed through the hole in the roof. I glanced at the hole to my left. I could see deeper into it, but there was no sign of it closing up. It just faded into dark shadows a long way down. To my right the slope angled away to the drop I had seen the previous night. Far away to the right of this sunlight sprayed against the back wall of the crevasse.

I picked absently at the frayed end of the rope, trying to come to a decision. I already knew that I wasn't prepared to spend another night on the ledge. I wasn't going through that madness again, but I cringed from doing the only thing left to me. I wasn't ready for such a choice. Without deciding I took some coils in hand, and then threw the rope down to the right. It flew clean out into space, and curled over the drop before falling out of sight. The rope jerked tight. I clipped my figure-of-eight to the rope, and lay on my side.

I hesitated, looking at the ice screw buried in the wall. It wouldn't pull free under my weight. The Prussik knot hung unused just below the ice screw. I thought that I should take it with me. If there was empty space at the end of the rope I would be unable to regain the ledge without it. I let myself slide off the ledge and watched the Prussik get smaller as I abseiled down the slope to the drop. If there was nothing there I didn't want to come back.

8

SILENT WITNESS

As I descended, the sense of menace threatened to overwhelm me. In contrast to the fury of the night before it was unnervingly quiet. I expected an avalanche to come hissing down but nothing moved. There wasn't a breath of wind to flurry the powder on the face, and even the snow kicked down by my steps slid away silently. It was as if the mountains were holding their breath, waiting for another death. Joe had died. The silence said so; but must they take me as well?

It was warm in the sun. The face caught its glare in the huge white bowl above me, and up there, thousands of feet above me, the snow shimmered in the heat. We had been up there yesterday but there was no trace of our passing. The night had swept it clean, and it waved gently in the heat haze. There was a dry foul taste in my mouth. Dehydration, no doubt; or a hollow bitterness rising. I stared at the mountain rising over me. Empty. It was a pointless thing to have done – climb up it, across it, and down it. Stupid! It looked perfect; so clean and untouched, and we had changed nothing. It was beautiful, immaculate, but it left me empty. I had been on it too long, and it had taken everything.

I continued the descent, stepping down with methodical precision. I could have moved quicker, but somehow there didn't seem to be any point. The windless silence closed over me. The glacier below my feet, encircled by ice mountains, remained quiet. There were no muffled ice collapses, or crevasses creaking open. I carried on down oppressed by the unnatural calm, and sensing that the hushed aura waited on

117

me. I would let it wait. I wanted to do this thing with calm, and dignity. The sense of menace grew heavier as I carefully retreated.

Crusts of snow slithered quickly over a drop below me. I was standing on the edge of an ice cliff. I leaned out from the slope and peered over the cliff at least 100 feet down. I raised my eyes and searched the glacier directly beneath the cliff for signs of life. There was nothing. No tell-tale signs of a snow hole. So this is what he went over. My God! Why this, here! We never knew. The dreadful suspicion that I had nursed through the night was confirmed. Joe was dead.

I stared at the glacier below in shocked silence. Although I had feared the worst I had never expected to find this. I had envisaged a small vertical wall, a rock buttress even, but not this towering ice cliff. I looked back up the face and marked the descent we had taken during the lowerings in a plumb straight line down to where I stood. I felt cheated. The very means by which we had managed to rescue ourselves had caused the accident. I remembered the mounting excitement I had felt as we had progressed smoothly down the mountain. I had been proud of what we had managed. It had worked so well – and all Joe's pain, all his digging, and fighting, had simply speeded the inevitable accident on the cliff. Over to the side I could make out the descent we had originally intended to take, descending diagonally to the left, away from the cliff. When we had decided on that line we hadn't noticed the ice cliff on the right. We had never imagined we would be lowering straight down.

I turned away from the drop and glared sightlessly at the peak directly in front of me. The cruelty of it all sickened me. It felt as if there were something deliberate about it, something preordained by a bored and evil force. The whole day's effort, and the chaos in the stormy night, had been for nothing. What fools we were to have thought we had been clever enough to get away with it! All that time struggling just to cut the rope. I laughed. The short bitter noise rang loud in the quiet. It was funny, I supposed. In a sick sort of way, it was funny all right, but the joke was on me. Some joke!

Faced into the snow slope, I began traversing the lip of the cliff. My fatalism had gone. Anger replaced it, and resentment, and with this bitter fury my lethargy disappeared. The resignation had been swept away. Although I felt weak and drained I was determined now to get off the mountain alive. It wasn't taking me as well.

Every now and then I glanced over the edge of the cliff. The further right I moved the shallower the cliff became, but the ground I was climbing over became increasingly steep and dangerous. Eventually the cliff face merged into the slope I was crossing, and the soft snow gave way to hard water ice with the occasional shattered rock protruding from it. I began to make a diagonal descent, moving very slowly. The climbing was technically demanding, so I found myself concentrating totally on what I was doing, and the emotions of earlier were forgotten.

After descending fifty feet I came to a rock frozen into the ice. I stood on the points of my crampons on 70° ice which was becoming harder and more brittle with every foot I descended. On closer inspection, I saw that I was on part of a rock buttress bulging out from under the ice. Glancing down, I saw that the ice rapidly thinned, and greyish shadows told me that the rock was only inches from the surface. I hammered a piton into a crack in the rock and clipped myself to it.

I found it awkward setting up the abseil. The rope was still frozen from the storm, and my numb fingers seemed to refuse to tie the knot for me. When it was done I threw the rope clear and it hung from the piton, dropping over the steep ground and reaching the easy slopes 150 feet below me. I fixed my belay plate to the rope, unclipped myself from the piton, and abseiled slowly down the ice-covered buttress.

As I moved down the rope the ice cliff gradually revealed itself. It stretched away to my left in a huge dome-shaped wall. At the top of the dome I saw where our ropes had cut deeply into the edge the previous night. They marked the highest point of the cliff. The face of the cliff was overhanging. The wall of white snow-ice loomed out from *the mountain, and the further I abseiled the more impending it became, until it seemed to hang over me despite the fact that I was well over to the right of it. I stared at it in amazement. It was huge, and I couldn't help but wonder why we had never noticed it. When we had approached the mountain we had walked across the glacier directly beneath it.*

It wasn't until I had descended half the rope's length that I glanced down and saw the crevasse. I jammed the belay plate shut, and stopped abruptly. I stared at the endless black depths at the foot of the cliff and shuddered in horror. Joe had undoubtedly fallen into the crevasse. I was appalled. The idea of falling into that monstrous blackness yawning below me made me grip the rope tightly. I shut my eyes and pressed my forehead against the taut rope.

For a long nauseous moment feelings of guilt and horror flooded through me. It was as if I had only just that minute cut the rope. I might as well have put a gun to his head and shot him. When I opened my eyes I couldn't look down at the crevasse and stared hopelessly at the rock-shadowed ice in front of me instead. Now that I was virtually clear of the mountain, and assured of my own survival, the full impact of what we had been through struck me. In the warm and peaceful sun the events of the previous night seemed so distant that I couldn't believe they had been so terrible. Everything had changed so much. I almost wished it were still as bad. At least then I would be fighting something. I would have reasons to justify my survival, and his end. As it was, I had only the stark blackness of the crevasse to accuse me.

I had never felt so wretchedly alone. I could not have won, and began to understand the reason for my dreadful sense of condemnation in the snow cave. If I hadn't cut the rope I would certainly have died. Looking at the cliff, I knew there would have been no surviving such a fall. Yet, having saved myself, I was now going to return home and tell people a story that few would ever believe. No one cuts the rope! It could never have been that bad! Why didn't you do this, or try that? I could hear the questions, and see the doubts in the eyes even of those who accepted my story. It was bizarre, and it was cruel. I had been on to a loser from the moment he broke his leg, and nothing could have changed it.

I tried to break from these useless thoughts by abseiling lower, staring into the crevasse, trying to see, desperately wanting to see, some sign of life. As I moved closer it grew wider, and the depths gained perspective, and loomed deeper. I kept staring in but my brief hopes faded with every foot descended. No one could have survived a fall into such depths, and even if Joe had there was nothing I could do for him. There was not enough rope here, or at camp, to reach down so deep. I knew also that I had no strength for such a task. It would be a vain and hopeless act to go down into the crevasse, and I was no longer prepared to face such risks. I had had enough of dying.

'JOE!'

I shouted, but the sound echoed in the blackness, mocking my puny effort.

It was too big, and the truth too stark. I couldn't try to believe he was alive. Everything told me otherwise, and any efforts I made to the contrary were just so much conscience-salving. I had looked into that awful hole, and shouted into it. In return I heard an echo and then an absolute silence that said everything I already knew.

My feet touched the snow. The abseil was over, and below me a slope ran smoothly down to the glacier. Another 200 feet would see me safely on it. I turned and looked up the ice cliff. I was at its extreme right-hand and slightly below the outer lip of the crevasse. The rope marks were still visible at the top of the cliff, mute testament to what I had done. Some fine powder snow fell from the cliff top in a gauzy white cloud. I watched it drift softly down. This place was ageless and lifeless. A mass of snow, and ice, and rock slowly moving upwards; freezing, thawing, cracking asunder, always changing with the passing of centuries. What a silly thing to pit oneself against! The snow cloud settled on the roofed area of the crevasse further to my left. Joe had fallen through there.

121

At least it had hidden his body from me, though I doubted I would have been able to see so far down.

I turned away, suppressing the idea of going back up for a second look. There was no point. There had to come a time for facing the truth. I couldn't stand there all day searching for a corpse. I faced the glacier and heeled down towards it feeling dazed.

When I reached the level snow of the glacier I dropped my sack in the snow and sat down. For a long time I stared bleakly at my boots, not wanting to look back at the mountain. The sense of security was overwhelming. I had made it! I just sat there thinking about the mountain, and all the days we had spent on it. I felt as if I were reviewing a year of my life, not six days. The glacier, walled in by ice faces, was a furnace of sun. Painfully white, it absorbed the heat from all sides and seemed to focus it on to me. I had taken off my jacket, over-trousers and thermal top without thinking. My actions had become automatic. The climbing and abseiling had happened without deliberate decision on my part. It was as if I had suddenly been transplanted to the glacier without any conscious effort, and my memory of the day's events had already faded into a blur of emotions and shocked thoughts. It was then that I realised how desperately tired I had become. The lack of food and water in the last twenty-four hours had taken its toll. Looking back at the ice cliff, which now seemed one small feature on a vast face, I knew I would never be able to get back up there. I wondered whether I would even manage to get to base camp. It would take days to eat, rest, and recover enough to mount a rescue attempt. Perhaps it's for the best then, Joe. At least you're dead. I almost spoke aloud to the distant ice cliff. The thought of finding him alive and terribly injured horrified me. I would have had to leave him to fetch help, but there was no help. When I was strong enough to return he would have died some desperate lonely death in the ice.

'Yes. It's best this way,' I whispered.

I trudged through the softened snow on the glacier, keeping

my back to Siula Grande. I could feel its presence massed behind me, and yearned to turn and look at it again. I kept walking, head-down, staring fixedly at the snow until I reached the crevasses at the end of the glacier. The ice had twisted and fractured in hundreds of parallel crevasses as the glacier ground up against the rock moraines. Some crevasses were easily seen and avoided, but many were covered with snow. Rolling smooth slopes hid the dangers below, and without a rope I felt naked and vulnerable.

The early-morning paranoia returned with a vengeance. In a foggy daze of heat and thirst I had forgotten the line we had taken when we approached the mountain. The first feelings of panic built up as I stared wildly from one crevasse to another. Had we gone above or below that one? Or was it that lower one? I couldn't remember. The harder I tried the more confused I became, and eventually I was weaving a contorted and terrifying path, unsure of where I was heading. Only the few feet of surrounding snow concerned me, and I moved aimlessly across the slopes, zigzagging, sometimes back-tracking, and at any moment I expected the snow to open a black emptiness beneath my feet.

When I reached the moraines I slumped down against a rock with my sack as a pillow, feeling the hot sun on my face as the fear of the crevasses melted away.

Raging thirst eventually forced me to my feet, and I stumbled unsteadily towards the widening boulder-strewn river which ran down from the moraines to the lakes above our camp. It was about four and a half miles to base, say a couple of hours' walking. I knew I could find water half-way down where melting snow streamed over a huge rounded granite boulder, and that was all I wanted. I could smell the water all around me. It trickled between boulders at my feet, and deeper in the crevices below the boulders I could hear it gurgling in full flow, yet unreachable.

After a few yards I stopped and turned for a last look at Siula Grande. I could see most of it but was thankful that the lower reaches were hidden by the curve of the glacier. I couldn't see the ice cliff. He was up there buried in the snow, but I no longer felt guilty about it. If I were ever in the same position again I felt certain I would act in the same way. Instead there was a slow ache inside, a growing sense of loss, and sorrow. This is what it had all come down to – standing alone amid the mountain debris thinking of the waste and the pity. I thought of saying a quiet farewell as I turned to leave, but in the end didn't. He had gone for good. The steady surge of the glacier would take him down to the valleys in the coming years, but by then he would have become a casual memory. Already, it seemed, I was beginning to forget him.

I stumbled through the chaotic maze of boulders and scree. When at last I looked back at the glacier, Siula Grande was no longer visible. I sagged wearily against a boulder, letting my mind run haphazardly over my pain and sorrow. The thirst had become unbearable. My mouth was dry and I swallowed. What little saliva it produced failed to ease the discomfort. The descent had become a confused blur of endless boulder fields, burning midday sun, and the thirst. My legs felt weighted down and so weakened I fell repeatedly among the rocks. When loose rocks slipped suddenly under my feet, I found that I had no strength to prevent myself falling. I used the axe to steady myself, and occasionally flung a hand out for support. Fingers slapped unfeeling against sharp boulders. The sun had failed to revive any sensation in them, and they remained numb and cold. After an hour I saw the rounded boulder, with water glistening as it ran over its flank. I quickened my pace, feeling a burst of energy come through me at the thought of water.

When I reached the hollow at the base of the boulder, and dropped my rucksack on the wet scree, I saw that there was not enough flow to satisfy my craving thirst. Carefully I built a catchment area in the gravel at the base of the rock. It filled with tantalising slowness and, after sucking a gritty mouthful, was empty again. I crouched at the rock drinking and waiting, and drinking again. There seemed no end to the amount I could drink. A sudden clatter from above made me duck away to the side. A handful of rocks thumped into the scree beside *me. I hesitated before returning to the water pool. We had rested and drunk from here on the way up. Rocks had also fallen on us then, and we had jumped away laughing at our fright. Joe had called it 'Bomb Alley'. The melting snow above the boulder released regular bombardments of small rocks as the day heated up.*

I sat on my sack spitting bits of grit from my mouth. There were footprints in the soft muddy scree and gravel of the hollow, the only trace left of our attempt on the mountain. It was a lonely place to rest. In the huge chaos of the moraines I had sat down to rest at the one spot where I would be reminded. We had sat in the same spot six days earlier. All our keen excitement, and the healthy strong feel in our bodies, had become an empty memory. I glanced at the moraines which hid the lower lake. There was little time left for this loneliness. I would reach base camp in another hour, and then it would be finished.

I set off for the lakes, the water flooding a fresh strength into my limbs. I was worried now by the thought of meeting Richard, who would want to know what had happened. Everyone would want to know. I didn't want to face the prospect of telling him. If I told him the truth I would be forced to tell the same story when I returned to home. All I could think about was the disbelief and criticism I was inevitably going to be confronted with. I couldn't face it. I shouldn't have to face it! Anger and guilt clashed in my arguments as to what I should do. I knew above everything that I had been right to do what I had done. Deep inside I would always know that I had nothing to be ashamed of. If I concealed the truth it wouldn't be so bad. I would be avoiding a lot of unnecessary pain and anguish.

Why tell them that you cut the rope? They'll never know otherwise, so what difference does it make! Just say he fell down a crevasse when we were coming down the glacier. Yeah! Tell them we were unroped. I know it's a stupid thing to do, but damn it, loads of climbers die like that. He's dead. How he died isn't important. I didn't kill. It's lucky I'm here at all . . . so why make it worse. I can't tell the truth.

125

God! I hardly believe it myself . . . they certainly won't.

When I reached the lake I was still convincing myself that to tell the truth was stupid. I knew it would only cause me grief. I could scarcely bear to think what Joe's parents would say. After drinking again at the lake I walked on towards camp more slowly. My mind kept telling me what I should say. It was reasonable and sensible. I couldn't fault the logic. But something inside shied away from doing it. Perhaps it was guilt. However many times I persuaded myself that I had no choice but to cut the rope a nagging thought said otherwise. It seemed like a blasphemy to have done such a thing. It went against every instinct; even against self-preservation.

The time passed without notice. I had wrapped myself in tangled hurtful thoughts until I felt I must surely burst. I could listen to no rational arguments against the feelings of guilt and cowardice which insisted so painfully. With the same fatalism as before I resigned myself to punishment. It seemed right to be punished; to atone for leaving him dead as if simply surviving had been a crime in itself. My friends would believe me and understand. The others could choose to think what they wished, and if it hurt me, well perhaps I deserved it.

At the end of the second small lake I climbed the final rise of the moraines and looked down on the two tents at base camp. The thought of food and drink and medication for my frostbite made me hurry down the cactus-covered hillside above the tents. I had forgotten about the dilemma of what to say to Richard and was almost running in my haste to get down. I slowed down to scramble over a small hillock, from the top of which I saw Richard walking slowly towards me. He was carrying a small rucksack and was bent over looking at the ground. He hadn't heard me. I stood still, shocked by his sudden appearance, and waited for him to come to me. An awful weariness rushed through me as I waited silently. It was all over, and the relief flooding me deepened the sense of exhaustion. I felt as if I were going to cry but my eyes remained stubbornly dry.

Richard looked up from the path and saw me. His anxious expression changed to surprise, and then he grinned broadly, his eyes alight with pleasure as he hurried to me:

'Simon! It's good to see you. I was worried.'

I could think of nothing to say and stared blankly at him. He looked confused and searched behind me for some sign of Joe. Perhaps my face told him, or he had been expecting something bad!

'Joe? . . .'

'Joe's dead.'

'Dead?'

I nodded. We fell silent. We couldn't look at each other. I dropped my sack to the ground and sat heavily on it, feeling as if I would never be able to stand up again.

'You look terrible!'

I didn't reply. I was thinking about what to say to him. My plan to lie was all very well but I couldn't summon enough energy to tell it. I stared at my blackened fingers helplessly.

'Here, eat this.' He handed me a bar of chocolate. 'I've got a stove, I'll get some tea going. I was just coming up to look for you. I thought you were lying hurt somewhere . . . Did Joe fall? What's happened . . .'

'Yeah, he fell,' I said flatly. 'There was nothing I could do.'

He chattered on nervously. I think he sensed that I needed time to adjust. I watched him preparing the tea, passing me more food, and searching in the medicine bag he had brought up. Eventually he gave it to me and I took it without saying anything. I felt a sudden deep affection and gratitude to him for being there. I knew he would have killed himself in the crevasses on the glacier if he had managed to get that far. I wondered whether he had been aware of the danger. He glanced up and saw me watching him. We smiled at each other.

It was warm sitting on the hillock. Without realising I was doing it I told Richard exactly what had happened. I could have done nothing else. He sat silently listening to all that I had been through, not once questioning me, nor looking surprised at what I was saying to him. I was glad I was telling him the truth. Not to have done so might have saved me hurt, but I knew as I told him that there was so much more we had managed to do that should be told. The rescue in the storm, the way we had worked together, the way we fought to get down alive. I couldn't say Joe had fallen into a crevasse when stupidly walking unroped on the glacier, not after he had been through so much trying to survive. I couldn't do him the injustice of lying, and my feeling of having failed him made it an impossibility to lie. When I had finished Richard looked at me:

'I knew something terrible had happened. I'm just glad you managed to get down.'

We packed away the remains of his provisions, and he put them in my big sack and then shouldered both sacks. We walked quietly down to the tents.

For me the rest of the day passed in a sluggish haze. I lay wearily in the sun outside the dome tent with my gear scattered around me drying in the sun. We talked no more of Joe. Richard busied himself producing a hot meal and endless cups of tea. Then he sat near me and talked of the long wait he had endured, gradually accepting that some disaster had overtaken us until he could bear the uncertainty no longer and had set out to find us. For six or seven hours I did nothing but doze and eat in the sun. It was difficult to adjust to the luxury of camp. I could feel my strength returning and lay in half sleep feeling my body mending itself.

Towards early evening the clouds massed in from the east, and the first heavy raindrops spattered us. There was a heavy roll of thunder and we retreated to the big dome tent which up until then I had been reluctant to enter. Richard brought his sleeping bag over from his tent and began cooking another meal on two gas stoves in the entrance. By the time we had finished eating the rain had turned to snow and a strong wind was shaking the tent. It was freezing outside.

We lay side by side in our sleeping bags listening to the storm. The candlelight flickered red and green off the tent walls, and by it I saw Joe's possessions shoved untidily to the back of the tent. I thought of the storm the previous night and

*shuddered. The picture remained in my head as I fell asleep.
I knew how bad it would be up there. The avalanches would
be pouring down, filling the crevasse at the ice cliff, burying
him. I fell into an exhausted dreamless sleep.*

9

IN THE FAR DISTANCE

The snow made soft rustling noises as it slithered into the depths below. I stared at the ice screw far above me, watching it getting smaller. The ice bridge which had stopped my fall stood out clearly. Behind it the open cavern of the crevasse faded into shadows. I gripped the rope gently, and let it slide through the belay plate at a smooth constant rate.

The desire to stop abseiling was almost unbearable. I had no idea what lay below me, and I was certain only of two things: Simon had gone and would not return. This meant that to stay on the ice bridge would finish me. There was no escape upwards, and the drop on the other side was nothing more than an invitation to end it all quickly. I had been tempted, but even in my despair I found that I didn't have the courage for suicide. It would be a long time before cold and exhaustion overtook me on the ice bridge, and the idea of waiting alone and maddened for so long had forced me to this choice: abseil until I could find a way out, or die in the process. I would meet it rather than wait for it to come to me. There was no going back now, yet inside I was screaming to stop.

I could not bring myself to look down to see what lay below. I dared not risk turning to discover just another deep hole. If I saw that I would stop immediately, and then what? A desperate struggle to remain on the rope fighting against the steep pull of the slope, unable to regain the ice bridge, but frantically trying to hang on as long as possible . . . No! I couldn't look down. I wasn't that brave. In fact I was having enough difficulty staving off the dread which swamped through me as I descended. It was this, or nothing . . . I had decided that on the bridge, and now I was committed. If it was to end here then I wanted it to be sudden and unexpected, so I kept my eyes fixed on the ice screw far above me.

The slope became steeper. When I was about fifty feet below the ice screw I felt my legs swing suddenly beneath me into open space. My grip stopped the rope involuntarily. This was the drop I had seen from the bridge! I stared up at the bridge trying to make myself release the rope again. I had experienced the sensation in the past, standing on the edge of a high diving board watching the water drops falling free from my hair to the pool below as I waged a mental battle to convince myself that there was nothing to it, daring myself to do it, and then off into space with a heart-stopping swoop, and laughter as I plunged safely into the water below. The knowledge that I could abseil until the rope ran out, and then fall into space as its unknotted end whipped through the belay plate, made me clench the rope even harder with my frozen hand. At last I released it and the old feeling – that the pool might suddenly move to one side, or the water empty as soon as I dived – returned once more, though I didn't know this time if there was a pool to aim for.

I abseiled slowly over the drop until I was hanging vertically on the rope. The wall of the drop was hard, clear, water ice. I could no longer see the ice screw, so I stared into the ice as I continued to lower myself past the wall. For a short while it held my attention, but as the light around me grew fainter the dread spilled over and I could contain myself no longer. I stopped.

I wanted to cry but couldn't. I felt paralysed, incapable of thinking, as waves of panic swept through me. The torment of anticipating something unknown and terribly frightening broke free, and for a helpless immeasurable time I hung shaking on the rope with my helmet pressed to the ice wall and my eyes tightly closed. I had to see what was beneath me because, for all my convictions, I didn't have the courage to do it blind. Surely it could not make me any more frightened.

I glanced at the rope stretched tautly above me. It ran up the wall and disappeared on to the slope above. There was no possibility of getting back to that slope some twenty feet above me. I looked at the wall of the crevasse close by my shoulder. On the other side another wall of ice towered up ten feet away. I was hanging in a shaft of water ice. The decision to look down came as I was in the process of turning. I swung round quickly, catching my smashed knee on the ice wall and howling in a frenzy of pain and fright. Instead of seeing the rope twisting loosely in a void beneath me, I stared blankly at the snow below my feet not fully believing what I was seeing. A floor! There was a wide snow-covered floor fifteen feet below me. There was no emptiness, and no black void. I swore softly, and heard it whisper off the walls around me. Then I let out a cry of delight and relief which boomed round the crevasse. I yelled again and again, listening to the echoes, and laughed between the yells. I was at the bottom of the crevasse.

When I recovered my wits I looked more carefully at the carpet of snow above which I was dangling. My jubilation was quickly tempered when I spotted dark menacing holes in the surface. It wasn't a floor after all. The crevasse opened up into a pear-shaped dome, its sides curving away from me to a width of fifty feet before narrowing again. The snow floor cut through the flat end of this cavern, while the walls above me tapered in to form the thin end of the pear barely ten feet across and nearly 100 feet high. Small fragments of crusty snow pattered down from the roof.

I looked round the enclosed vault of snow and ice, familiarising myself with its shape and size. The walls opposite closed in but didn't meet. A narrow gap had been filled with snow from above to form a cone which rose all the way to the roof. It was about fifteen feet wide at the base and as little as four or five feet across at the top.

A pillar of gold light beamed diagonally from a small hole in the roof, spraying bright reflections off the far wall of the crevasse. I was mesmerised by this beam of sunlight burning through the vaulted ceiling from the real world outside. It had me so fixated that I forgot about the uncertain floor below and let myself slide down the rest of the rope. I was going to reach that sunbeam. I knew it then with absolute certainty. How I would do it, and when I would reach it were not considered. I just knew.

In seconds my whole outlook had changed. The weary frightened hours of night were forgotten, and the abseil which had filled me with such claustrophobic dread had been swept away. The twelve despairing hours I had spent in the unnatural hush of this awesome place seemed suddenly to have been nothing like the nightmare I had imagined. I could do something positive. I could crawl and climb, and keep on doing so until I had escaped from this grave. Before, there had been nothing for me to do except lie on the bridge trying not to feel scared and lonely, and that helplessness had been my worst enemy. Now I had a plan.

The change in me was astonishing. I felt invigorated, full of energy and optimism. I could see possible dangers, very real risks that could destroy my hopes, but somehow I knew I could overcome them. It was as if I had been given this one blessed chance to get out and I was grasping it with every ounce of strength left in me. A powerful feeling of confidence and pride swept over me as I realised how right I had been to leave the bridge. I had made the right decision against the worst of my fears. I had done it, and I was sure that nothing now could be worse than those hours of torture on the bridge.

My boots touched the snow and I stopped descending. I sat in my harness, hanging free on the rope a few feet from the floor, and examined the surface cautiously. The snow looked soft and powdery, and I was immediately suspicious of it. I looked along the edge where the floor joined the walls and soon found what I was looking for. In several places there were dark gaps between the ice walls and the snow. It was not a floor so much as a suspended ceiling across the crevasse dividing the abyss below from the upper chamber where I sat. The start of the snow slope running up to the sunshine lay forty feet from me. The inviting snow-carpet between me and the slope tempted me to run across it. The idea made me chuckle. I had forgotten that my right leg was useless. Okay. Crawl across it . . . but which way? Straight across, or keeping near to the back wall?

It was a difficult decision. I was less worried about putting my foot through the floor than by the damage such a fall would do to the fragile surface. The last thing I wanted was to destroy the floor and leave myself stranded on the wrong side of an uncrossable gap. That would be too much to bear. I glanced nervously at the beam of sunlight, trying to draw strength from it, and made my mind up at once. I would cross in the middle. It was the shortest distance and there was nothing to suggest that it would be any riskier than at the sides. I gently lowered myself until I was sitting on the snow but with most of my weight still on the rope. It was agonising to inch the rope out and let my weight down gradually. I found myself holding my breath, every muscle in my body tensed. I became acutely aware of the slightest movement in the snow, and I wondered whether I would end up sinking slowly through the floor. Then some of the tension in the rope relaxed, and I realised that the floor was holding. I breathed deeply, and released my aching hand from the rope.

I sat very still for five minutes, trying to get used to the precarious feeling of being balanced above a huge drop by a fragile sheet of snow. I belatedly realised that it was something I couldn't adjust to and that there was no choice but to attempt to cross the gap. I let out forty feet of rope and tied the remaining thirty feet to my harness. Then, lying spreadeagled on my stomach, I began to wiggle stealthily towards the snow cone, anxiety easing as I got closer to the other side. An occasional muffled thumping told me that snow had fallen away into the drop beneath the floor. I would freeze rigidly at the slightest sound, holding my breath and feeling my heart hammering before moving off again. The black holes in the floor were all behind me when I passed the half-way point and I sensed that I was now crawling over thicker and stronger snow.

After ten minutes I lay slumped against the slope rising

towards the golden sun in the roof. The abseil rope hung in a curve before the ice wall and the steep slope above it running up to the ice bridge. If only I had known there was a floor down here I could have saved myself a lot of grief. The thought that I might have waited up there made me shudder. It would have been a drawn-out vigil of madness and cold. At the end I would have slipped into exhausted unconsciousness after enduring days of consuming despair.

I glanced up the snow cone. For a brief moment I wondered whether I had been deluding myself with the idea that I could possibly reach the sun above. It was a long way, and steep. I would be able to climb the slope while still tied to the rope. As I gained height the rope would rise with me until it hung almost horizontally between the snow bridge and the sun roof. A fall at any point would not prevent me from crashing straight through the floor, where I would swing in a pendulum in the lower cavern until I hit the ice wall down which I had abseiled. If that happened there would be no return to the snow cone, or the ice bridge. I thought of climbing without the rope. At least the end would be mercifully quick. I dismissed the idea. I needed the rope. It gave me a feeling of security.

A slight breeze ran through the crevasse and I felt it on my cheek, a chill, deathly brush from somewhere deep below me. The light in the chamber was a strange mix of blue-grey shadows and dancing reflections from the ice walls surrounding me. Rocks embedded in the walls stood out starkly in the wet translucent ice. I rested at the base of the snow cone, absorbing the feel of the crevasse. For all its hushed cold menace, there was a feeling of sacredness about the chamber, with its magnificent vaulted crystal ceiling, its gleaming walls encrusted with a myriad fallen stones, shadows facing into darkness beyond the great gateway formed by the ice bridge which hid the silent vault beyond. The menace was in my imagination but I couldn't stop it playing on my mind, as if this thing had waited for a victim with the impersonal patience of the centuries. It had me now, and without the sunbeam I might have sat there numbed and defeated by its implacable stillness. I shivered. The air was uncomfortably cold, was well below freezing. A puff of wind outside sprinkled powder through the hole in the roof, and I watched fascinated as it drifted in the sunlight. It was time to climb.

I stood up gingerly on my left leg letting my damaged limb hang uselessly above the snow. It had stiffened during the night and now hung shorter than my good leg. At first I wasn't sure how to set about climbing the slope, which I guessed to be 130 feet high – ten minutes' work with two legs. It was the angle of the slope that worried me. To begin with, it rose at an angle of only 45°, and I felt confident that I could drag myself up that, but as it gained height so the angle increased. The top twenty feet looked almost vertical, but I knew that my eyes were being confused by looking straight on to the slope. I decided it could be no more than 65° at the top. The thought wasn't encouraging: loose powder would be exhausting enough without the injury. I suppressed a growing pessimism by telling myself that I was lucky to have found a slope at all.

The initial steps were clumsy and unco-ordinated. I dug my ice axes deep into the snow above me and then hauled myself up the snow with my arms. It wouldn't work on the steeper slope above, and I realised how risky it was. If an axe ripped free of the snow I would fall. I stopped and tried to work out a better method. My knee throbbed painfully, harshly reminding me that I was a very long way from getting out.

Patterns! I remembered how I had traversed to the col with Simon. It seemed so long ago. That's the way. Find a routine and stick to it. I was resting on my axes looking at my good leg buried in the snow. I tried lifting the injured leg up parallel with it and groaned as the knee crunched and refused to bend properly, leaving the boot about six inches lower than the good foot. Pain flared up as I leant down and dug a step in the snow. I tamped it down as much as possible, then dug another smaller step below it. When I had finished I planted both axes in the slope above, gritted my teeth, and heaved my burning leg up until the boot rested in the lower step. Bracing myself on the axes, I made a convulsive hop off my good leg, pressing my arms hard down for extra thrust. A searing pain burst from my knee as my weight momentarily came on to it, and then faded as the good leg found a foothold on the higher step. I shouted an obscenity which echoed comically round the chamber. Then I bent down to dig another two steps and repeat the pattern. Bend, hop, rest; bend, hop, rest . . . The flares of pain became merged into the routine and I paid less attention to them, concentrating solely on the patterns. I was sweating profusely despite the cold. Agony and exertion blended into one, and time passed unnoticed as I became absorbed with the patterns of hopping and digging. I resisted the urge to look up or down. I knew that I was making desperately slow progress and I didn't want to be reminded of it by seeing the sunbeam still far above me.

After two and a half hours the slope had steepened considerably, and I had to be especially careful when I hopped. There was a critical moment when all my weight was on the axes driven into the loose snow, and the angle forced me to balance my movements precisely. I had nearly fallen on two occasions. One hop had missed the good step and I had slithered into the smaller step below, with my knee twisting beneath my weight. I had struggled to remain standing, fighting off the nausea and faintness. The second time I had hopped successfully but too explosively and had lost balance. Again I felt things move and grind in my knee as I swung violently forward into the snow to stop the fall. It was odd to curse and sob and hear the sounds repeated in the chamber below. Even more peculiar was the feeling of acute embarrassment at complaining like that. There was no one to hear, but the looming empty chamber behind me made me feel inhibited, as if it were some disapproving silent witness to my weakness.

I rested with my head against the snow. I was soaked in sweat but it cooled quickly when I stopped. Soon I was shivering. I glanced at the roof above and was delighted to see the sun nearly touching me. Looking down, I saw that I was two-thirds of the way up the snow cone. The chamber appeared even more cavernous from my high perch. The rope hung in a crescent from my harness to the ice screw at the ice bridge. I was level with the bridge, and the rope hung clear of the slope down which I had abseiled, stretching out eighty feet above the floor of the chamber below. Looking at the ice bridge, I felt disturbed at the memory of my time spent on it. It was hard to believe how desperate I had been in the night and while abseiling now that I was reaching for the sun. That was the hardest thing I had ever done, and thinking about it I felt a surge of confidence build in me. There was still a lot to fight for. I turned into the slope and began digging steps again.

It took another two and a half hours to reach a point ten feet below the hole in the roof. The angle of the snow had become almost impossibly difficult, and every hop had to be a measured gamble against losing balance and making the step. Fortunately the snow conditions improved as the cone narrowed and I found that I could get a solid axe placement in the ice wall to my left. I felt exhausted despite the approaching roof. The pain reached a level and then stayed constant. No amount of care could prevent the temporary weight I had to place on my knee, and I felt weak and sickened by the repeated twisted crunching spasms in the fracture site. I bent into the slope again and hopped, pulling up powerfully on the axe I had placed in the wall, and got my boot into the step without hurting the bad knee. The snow roof brushed my helmet. I was directly beneath the small head-sized hole in the snow. The glare from the sun was blinding, and when I looked down, the chamber had disappeared into inky darkness. I hefted my leg into the new step I had dug and prepared to make another hop.

If anyone had seen me emerge from the crevasse they would have laughed. My head popped up through the snow roof and I stared gopher-like at the scene outside. I kept hold of the axe planted in the wall of the crevasse and stood on one leg with my head stuck out of the snow, swivelling round to take in the most stupendous view I had ever seen. The ring of mountains surrounding the glacier were so spectacular that I hardly recognised what I was seeing. The familiar peaks had taken on a beauty I had never noticed before. I could see icefields and delicately fluted ridges, and a dark sea of moraines curled out of sight from the snout of the glacier. There wasn't a cloud in the sky, and the sun glared from its azure emptiness with ferocious heat. I stood silent and stunned, unable to accept that I was at last free again. My senses had been so battered that I had forgotten what to expect at this moment of escape.

I hauled my hammer from the crevasse and drove it into the snow outside. When I hopped and rolled out of the yawning drop, I lay against the snow numb with relief. I felt as if I had been fighting someone too strong for me for far too long. Though the sun warmed through my back I still shivered. The heavy weight of despair and fear which had been with me for so long in the ice chamber seemed to melt away in the sun. I lay inert on the snow with my face turned to the glacier below and my mind empty of thoughts. The relief washing through me left me light-headed and weak, as if I had used up the last reserve of energy within me. I didn't want to move and risk disturbing the contentment and peace of lying there motionless in the snow. The blessed relief from tension, and darkness, and nightmare images, was total. I realised then just how frantic I had been during every second of the past twelve hours and in response my mind shut itself off from all but the sensation of relaxing. I felt drowsy from the sun and wanted to sleep and forget. I had succeeded beyond my wildest hopes. I had escaped without ever thinking I could, and for the moment that was enough.

I did not sleep, but lay silent in a half-conscious limbo, slowly adjusting to my new world. I flicked my eyes from view to view without moving my head, registering the familiar landscape as if for the first time. The glacier, like a frozen tongue, curled away to the north and broke into a maze of crevasses on the black moraines at its snout. The moraines tumbled chaotically through a wide rocky valley until they thinned to mud and screes on the bank of a circular lake in the far distance. Another lake flashed sunlight off its surface just beyond the first. Sarapo blocked my view but I knew that the second lake ended at another bank of moraines, and beyond that lay the tents.

Slowly it dawned on me that my new world, for all its warmth and beauty, was little better than the crevasse. I was 200 feet above the glacier and six miles from base camp. The tranquility evaporated, and a familiar tension returned. The crevasse had been only a starter! How foolish to have thought that I had done it, that I was safe! I stared at the distant moraines and the glimmers of light from the lakes, and felt crushed. It was too far, too much. I wasn't strong enough. I had no food, no water, nothing, and again I felt the menace surrounding me. I almost believed that I wasn't going to be allowed to escape; whatever I did would lead to another barrier, and then another, until I stopped and gave in. The black moraines and glittering lake water in the distance mocked any hopes of escape. I was in a malevolent place; a tangible hostility enclosed me as if the air had been charged with static electricity. This was not the playground we had walked into so long ago.

I sat up and looked bitterly at the frayed rope-end which I had carried up from the crevasse.

'This is getting ridiculous,' I said aloud quietly, as if afraid something might hear me and know I was beaten.

As I gazed at the distant moraines I knew that I must at least try. I would probably die out there amid those boulders. The thought didn't alarm me. It seemed reasonable, matter-of-fact. That was how it was. I could aim for something. If I died, well, that wasn't so surprising, but I wouldn't have just waited for it to happen. The horror of dying no longer affected me as it had in the crevasse. I now had the chance to confront it and struggle against it. It wasn't a bleak dark terror any more, just fact, like my broken leg and frostbitten fingers, and I couldn't be afraid of things like that. My leg would hurt when I fell, and when I couldn't get up I would die. In a peculiar way it was refreshing to be faced with simple choices. It made me feel sharp and alert, and I looked ahead at the land stretching into distant haze and saw my part in it with a greater clarity and honesty than I had ever experienced before.

I had never been so entirely alone, and although this alarmed me it also gave me strength. An excited tingle ran down my spine. I was committed. The game had taken over, and I could no longer choose to walk away from it. It was ironic to have come here searching out adventure and then find myself involuntarily trapped in a challenge harder than any I had sought. For a while I felt thrilled as adrenalin boosted through me, but it couldn't drive away the loneliness or shorten the miles of moraines tumbling towards the lakes. The sight of what lay ahead soon killed the excitement. I was abandoned to this awesome and lonely place. It sharpened my perception to see clearly and sharply the facts behind the mass of useless thoughts in my head, and to realise how vital it was just to be there, alive and conscious, and able to change things. There was silence, and snow, and a clear sky empty of life, and me, sitting there, taking it all in, accepting what I must try to achieve. There were no dark forces acting against me. A voice in my head told me that this was true, cutting through the jumble in my mind with its coldly rational sound.

It was as if there were two minds within me arguing the toss. The *voice* was clean and sharp and commanding. It was always right, and I listened to it when it spoke and acted on its decisions. The other mind rambled out a disconnected series of images, and memories and hopes, which I attended to in a daydream state as I set about obeying the orders of the *voice*. I had to get to the glacier. I would crawl on the glacier, but I didn't think that far ahead. If my perspectives had sharpened, so too had they narrowed, until I thought only in terms of achieving predetermined aims and no further. Reaching the glacier was my aim. The *voice* told me exactly how to go about it, and I obeyed while my other mind jumped abstractedly from one idea to another.

I began a one-footed, hopping descent of the face below the crevasse. I headed diagonally to the right in order to by-pass a steep rock buttress which was directly beneath me. Once past it, I saw that the snow ran smoothly down 200 feet to the glacier. I glanced up at the ice cliff above the crevasse. It was a dim past memory, until I spotted the rope hanging down the right-hand side and knew with a sudden pang that Simon had also seen it. The string of colour hanging down the ice dispelled any doubts I might have still clung to. He had survived and seen the crevasse. He hadn't gone to get help; he had left in the certain knowledge that I was dead. I looked back to my feet and concentrated on hopping.

10

MIND GAMES

The snow was deep and the sun softened it. I planted the axes firmly into the snow and leant on them heavily while I executed a hasty downward hop-cum-kick. I had only one chance at making a secure step with the kick. The damaged leg hung slackly above the snow. Despite taking care, I often snagged it, or the sudden downward jolt would pull at the knee joint, making me cry out. When I next looked at the glacier I was pleased to see that it was about eighty feet from where I stood, and that there were no crevasses or bergschrunds between me and the bottom of the slope. The surface of the slope, however, was changing, and I was alarmed to see patches of bare ice a few feet below me. I managed two more hops before the inevitable happened. I knew it would and had prepared myself for it. As soon as I hopped on to the ice my crampons skittered off and I tumbled sideways. I fell head-first on my right side and tobogganed down the slope on my windproof jacket and trousers. My boots rattled over the ice, knocking my legs together, and producing flares of agony to which I responded with eyes closed and gritted teeth. It was short, fast and terribly painful.

When I came to a stop in a build-up of snow, I lay absolutely still while the pain throbbed up and down my leg. I tried to get the good leg off the bent-back injured knee, but as soon as I moved a dreadful stabbing made me scream and remain still. I raised myself and looked at my legs. The crampons on my right foot had caught in the gaiters of the good leg, so twisting my knee back in a familiar distorted shape. When I reached forward to free the spikes, fresh pain stabbed through my knee. I couldn't free them without bending further. Eventually I managed to unhook the spikes with an axe, and I laid my leg gently on to the snow, straightening the knee slowly until the agony faded.

I had come to a stop ten feet from a meandering line of footprints. I pulled myself over to them and rested. It was comforting to find the prints. I looked at their shadow marks trailing sinuously across the glacier towards a distant circular-shaped crevasse. The glacier rolled away from me in undulating waves of snow, and between the waves the tracks would disappear, only to reappear on the crest of the next wave. I needed the tracks. From my position, lying on the snow, I had a very limited view ahead and without the tracks I would have little idea of where I was heading. Simon knew the way down, and without a rope he would have taken the safest possible line. All I had to do was follow.

It took some experimentation before I found the best method of crawling. The soft wet snow made it hard to slide. I quickly realised that facing forwards on one knee and both arms was too painful. I lay on my left side, keeping the injured knee out of the way, and through a combination of pulling on axes and shoving with the left leg I made steady progress. The bad leg slid along behind like an unwanted pest. From time to time I stopped to eat snow and rest. Then I would stare vacantly at the huge West Face of Siula Grande above me and listen to the strange thoughts echoing in my head. Then the *voice* would interrupt the reverie and I would glance guiltily at my watch before starting off again.

The *voice*, and the watch, urged me into motion whenever the heat from the glacier halted me in a drowsy exhausted daze. It was three o'clock – only three and a half hours of daylight left. I kept moving but soon realised that I was making ponderously slow headway. It didn't seem to concern me that I was moving like a snail. So long as I obeyed the *voice*, then I would be all right. I would look ahead and note some features in the waves of snow, then look at my watch, and the *voice* told me to reach that point in half an hour. I obeyed. Sometimes I found myself slacking, sitting in a daydream, lost to what I was doing, and I would start up guiltily and try to make up time by crawling faster. It never let up. I crawled in a mechanical automatic daze because I was told that I must reach the prescribed spot in time.

As I inched over the sea of snow I listened to other voices that wondered what people were doing in Sheffield and remembered the thatched-cottage pub in Harome where I used to drink before the expedition. I hoped that Ma was praying for me as she always did, and at the memory of her my eyes blurred wetly with hot tears. I sang lyrics of a pop song incessantly to the tune of my crawling, and kept filling my head with countless thoughts and images until I stopped and sat swaying in the heat. Then the *voice* would tell me I was late, and I would wake with a start and crawl again. I was split in two. A cold clinical side of me assessed everything, decided what to do and made me do it. The rest was madness – a hazy blur of images so vivid and real that I lost myself in their spell. I began to wonder whether I was hallucinating.

A film of weariness enveloped everything. Events passed in slow motion, and thoughts became so confused I lost all sense of time passing. When I stopped I would make an excuse for it, so as not to feel guilty. My frostbitten fingers became the most common excuse. I had to take my mitts and inner gloves off to check that they were not getting worse. Ten minutes later the *voice* would jolt me back to reality, and I would pull on the glove I had only half managed to remove and tug my mitt over it, and crawl. My hands were always deep in the snow as I crawled, and when they had gone numb I would stop again and stare at them. I meant to massage them, or remove the gloves and heat them in the sun, but I just stared at them blankly until the *voice* called me.

After two hours the circular crevasse was behind me and I had escaped the shadow of Siula Grande. I followed the footprints in a crescent under Yerupaja's South Face, passing the broken side of a crevasse which thrust out from the glacier snow. It was only fifty feet long but I passed it like a ship passes an iceberg. I drifted slowly by, staring at the bared ice.

I seemed to be drifting with it on a current. It didn't strike me as odd that I wasn't overtaking the ice cliff. I gazed at figures in the broken ice of the cliff. I was unsure whether I could really see them. Voices argued with the commanding *voice*, and decided I was seeing them. They reminded me of an old man's head I had once seen in a cloud while lying on a beach. My friend couldn't see it, which had made me angry, because even if I looked away and then back at the cloud I could still see the old man, so it had to be there. It looked like a Renaissance painting, in the Sistine Chapel, where the white-bearded old man pointing his finger from the ceiling was supposed to be God.

There was nothing pious about the figures I watched in the ice. Many figures, some half formed, all frozen in bas-relief, stood out starkly from the cliff face. Sun shadows and colours in the ice gave them solidity. All were copulating. I was fascinated, and crawled steadily as I gawped at the obscene figures in the ice. I had seen these figures before as well. They reminded me of pictures I had seen of the carvings inside a Hindu temple. There was no order in the chaos of figures. They stood, or kneeled, or were lying down. Some were upside-down and I had to cock my head to make out what they were doing. It was funny and titillating, like the paintings by Titian of grossly fat nudes that had mesmerised me at fourteen.

A short while later I sat still in the snow with a mitt in my lap, tugging at an inner glove with my teeth. The cliff was no longer in sight. Between seeing the figures and stopping to check my fingers I had no memory of doing anything. One moment I was looking at the ice figures, the next I was alone again and the cliff, mysteriously, was behind me. A spray of icy snow crystals stung my face. The wind was getting up. I looked at the sky and was surprised to see that a rolling carpet of heavy cumulus had covered the sun. Another gust of wind made me turn my face away. A storm was building. It was cold in the wind, which had sprung up from nowhere and now buffeted me with increasing force. I hurriedly pulled on my mitt and turned to face the footprints.

I was less dazed now, and the *voice* had banished the mad thoughts from my mind. An urgency was creeping over me, and the *voice* said: '*Go on, keep going ... faster. You've wasted too much time. Go on, before you lose the tracks,*' and I tried hard to hurry. The wind gusted fine clouds across the glacier ahead of me. They swirled low over the surface. Sometimes they covered me and I could see no more than a few yards, but if I sat up I could see over fine spindrift that scooted across the glacier, making it look as if the glacier were rushing forward in whirls and eddies. I wondered what people would think to see this head and torso sticking out from the glacier. I lay on my side and crawled in fast bursts, before popping my head above the stormy curtain again to peer forward. There was snow in the air above. Fresh falling snow! My stomach tightened as panic threatened. The snow and wind would hide the footprints. The *voice* said I would lose my way, said I would never get through the crevasses without the prints, and told me to hurry on, but what I was really frightened of was losing a sign of life in the empty bowl of mountains surrounding me. I had followed the footprints happily, as if Simon were just up ahead and I wasn't alone. Now the wind and snow threatened to leave me utterly alone. I clawed feverishly through the gusting snow, squinting ahead at the rapidly fading tracks.

The light faded quickly. Night was approaching and with it the wind grew stronger. I didn't waste time warming my frozen hands, but urgently followed the soft marks of filled-in footprints until I could see no more. It was dark. I lay face down in the snow defeated. The strenuous crawling had warmed me and I could lie still feeling the wind pushing snow up around me without being cold. I wanted to sleep. I couldn't be bothered to move any more. I was warm enough sleeping on the snow. The storm would cover me like a husky and keep me warm. I nearly slept, dozing fitfully, edging close to the dark comfort of sleep, but the wind kept waking me. I tried to ignore the *voice,* which urged me to move, but couldn't because the other voices had gone. I couldn't lose the *voice* in daydreams.

147

'. . . *don't sleep, don't sleep, not here. Keep going. Find a slope and dig a snow hole . . . don't sleep.*'

The darkness and the storm confused me. I lost track of how long I moved through the snow, and even forgot that I was on a glacier with crevasses all around me. I kept crawling forward blindly. Once there was a roaring, louder than the wind, and a sudden blast of ice fragments hit me. An avalanche, or a cornice falling from Yerupaja into the glacier. I registered that it hit me, its force spent, and swept over me. Then the wind noise returned and I forgot the avalanche. It never occurred to me that I might have been in danger.

Suddenly I rolled forward and fell. In the dark I couldn't make out what I had slid into with a rush. As I came to a stop, I turned and faced the way I had come. There was a bank of snow above me, and I groped my way back up it, dragging at the snow with my axes, hopping and crying out with the pains in my knee.

I dug the snow hole in a confusion of pain and exhaustion. As I burrowed into the bank I was forced to twist and turn to enlarge the hole, so wrenching my knee excruciatingly from side to side.

The other voices returned once I was sheltered from the wind, and I dozed off with their images idly flitting through my mind. I jolted awake and started digging to the repeated tune of a song in my head, then dozed, then back to my voices.

I fumbled in my rucksack with unfeeling hands for my head-torch. I pulled my sleeping bag from the sack and found the torch inside. With its feeble dying light I saw that the cave wasn't long enough for me to lie stretched out, but I was too tired to carry on digging. Leaning forward to remove my crampons put unbearable pressure on my damaged knee. I groaned and sobbed with frustration as my deadened fingers flicked ineffectually over the heel-release bar. I couldn't grip the bar hard enough to pull the crampon from my boot. I was bent double over my legs trying to avoid breaking through the roof of the cave with my head and cried with pain and impotent fury. I stopped pulling at the bar and sat quietly until the idea to use my axe came to me. The bar on each boot popped off easily with the leverage from the axe. I lay back in the cave and dozed.

Hours seemed to pass before I had laid out the insulation mat and struggled into my sleeping bag. Hefting my broken leg into the bag was awkward and pain-wracked. The boot snagged on the wet fabric of the bag, jerking fire from the knee joint. My leg felt amazingly heavy when I lifted it into the bag, and it felt dead and lumpy. It got in the way like a pestering child, making me irritable, as if it were something I ordered around and it stubbornly refused to obey.

There was no sound of the storm raging outside. Occasionally I felt the wind tug at the end of the sleeping bag protruding from the entrance, and then this also fell quiet as the snow covered my feet and sealed the cave. I checked my watch. Ten-thirty. I knew I must sleep, yet now that it was safe to sleep I felt sharply awake. Memories of the crevasse came back in the dark of the cave and forced hopes of sleep away. My knee throbbed unmercifully. I worried about getting frostbitten feet, and thought of my fingers. It occurred to me that I might not wake up if I fell asleep, so I kept my eyes open and stared into the dark. I knew I was being scared unnecessarily by such thoughts now that it was dark and I had nothing more to do, but it didn't help.

Eventually I slept in a dreamless black stupor. The night was long and silent while the storm blew itself out on the snows above me, and from time to time pain and childish fears ambushed my sleep.

It was late when I awoke. The sun glowed through the tent walls, making me uncomfortably hot in my sleeping bag. I lay motionless, staring at the domed roof. It seemed incredible that at this time yesterday I had been stumbling through the crevasses at the end of the glacier. Joe had been dead thirty-six hours. I felt as if he had been gone for weeks, yet it was only seven days since we had set off together up the mountain. There was a hollow ache inside which no food could fill; it would pass with time. Already he was a vaguely recollected memory. It was strange how I couldn't picture his face in my mind. So, he was gone, and there was nothing I could do to change it. I fumbled with numb fingers to release the sleeping-bag drawcord, shuffled it off me, and went out to the sun. I was hungry.

Richard was busy priming the petrol stove by the cooking rock. He glanced at me and smiled. It was a beautiful day; one of those days to make you feel good and zestful. I went to the river bed and urinated on a boulder. Sarapo loomed in front of me but its spectacular beauty no longer interested me. I was bored with this place and these pretty views. There was no point in being here. It was barren and lifeless; I hated the place for its cruelty, and for what it had made me do. I wondered whether I had murdered him.

I walked back to Richard and hunkered down beside him in a black despairing mood. He silently handed me a cup of tea and a bowl of milky porridge. I ate quickly and tasted little. When I had finished I walked over to the tent, collected my washing things and made my way to a deep pool in the river. I stripped off and stepped into the freezing water, dipping myself hurriedly under and gasping as the cold took my breath away. The sun dried me and warmed my back as I shaved. I spent a long time by the pool, cleaning my clothes and picking at the sunburn on my face. It was a peaceful, cleansing ritual and my despair gradually faded as I mulled over the past few days. When I walked back to the tents it was with a fresh spirit. It had happened and I had done everything possible. Okay, he was dead and I wasn't, but that was no reason for tormenting myself. I had to get things straight in my own mind before I could return and face the inevitable criticism. I knew that once I had accepted it all then I could tell others. They would never know what it had been like, and I doubted whether I could ever articulate it, even to close friends, but I didn't have to so long as it felt right inside. The healing process had started. For the moment I was content.

Richard had left the camp when I returned. I searched round the tent looking for the medicine box. It lay partly hidden by some of Joe's clothes at the back of the tent. I threw it on to the grass outside and then sifted through his things.

After fifteen minutes there was a pile of clothes and possessions lying in the sun by the medicines. I sat beside them, opened the medicine kit and began systematically to dose myself. I swallowed Ronicols, to improve the circulation in my fingers and prevent the frostbite taking too deep a hold. Wide-spectrum antibiotics followed, to combat infection. Then another drawn-out session of picking, cleaning and inspecting followed. It was wonderfully restorative. The ritualised examination seemed to confirm to me that everything was back to normal. It was a luxury and a balm. Feet, fingers, face, hair, chest and legs – all got the treatment.

When I had finished I turned to the pile of possessions and began sorting through them. I placed all his clothes in one pile and laid out his possessions in a line to one side. I felt quite calm and mechanical as I separated them. I found his used film and a zoom lens in a plastic bag. It was a large bag so I gathered all the things I wanted to give to his parents and put them in as well. There wasn't much.

I found his diary. He had written something almost every day, even on the plane from London. He liked writing. I glanced through it but didn't read the words. I didn't want to know what he had said. I ignored what climbing equipment he had left behind. It was of no value to anyone but a climber. I would pack it home with my gear. When I turned to his clothes I flicked through them quickly. I soon found his hat. It was a black-and-white patterned woolly hat with its bobble missing. I knew he had really liked it, and I placed it in the bag with the rest. It came from Czechoslovakia. Miri Smidt had given it to him in Chamonix. I couldn't bring myself to burn it.

Richard came back just as I had finished with what I would give to Joe's parents. He fetched some petrol and we burnt the clothes in the river bed. The trousers wouldn't burn well and we had to use a lot of petrol. Richard had suggested we should give them to the girls and the kids down in the valley. They would have liked to have them, as their clothes were so tattered, but I went ahead and burnt them.

When it was over we returned to the cooking rock and sat

quietly in the sun. Richard made a hot meal and provided endless cups of tea. We played cards or listened to music on the personal stereos. Richard went and fetched Joe's stereo from the plastic bag because his was broken, and the day passed idly. When we talked it was quietly and about home or future plans. The hollow feeling was still with me and the guilt which I knew I could never erase, but I could deal with it now.

11

A LAND WITHOUT PITY

I awoke screaming. It was light in the snow cave, and cold. The nightmare subsided slowly and I remembered where I was. It wasn't the crevasse. The relief washed over me as I tried to forget the dream. I lay still, looking at the rough snow roof above me. It was deathly quiet, and I wondered whether the storm was still raging above me. I didn't want to move. It was going to hurt after the long cold night. I twitched my leg gingerly and was rewarded with a stab of sharp pain from my knee. My breath clouded on to the snow roof and I watched it vacantly.

The dream had been so vividly clear that I had believed it to be true. I had seen myself back on the ice bridge, crumpled against the crevasse wall, sobbing. I saw myself sobbing but could hear no sounds. Instead a voice, my voice, recited a soliloquy from Shakespeare over and over again:

> Ay, but to die and go we know not where;
> To lie in cold obstruction and to rot;
> This sensible warm motion to become
> A kneaded clod . . .

I was awake now, and knew exactly where I was, but the words still echoed in my head, and I remembered where I had learnt them. Ten years ago I had recited those words in just the same parrot fashion, over and over again I had said them aloud in my room, trying to memorise them word-perfectly for the O-Level literature exam in the morning. I was astounded. I hadn't read the lines since that time and yet now I could remember every word:

> . . . and the delighted spirit
> To bathe in fiery floods, or to reside
> In thrilling region of thick-ribbed ice;
> To be imprison'd in the viewless winds,
> And blown with restless violence round about
> The pendant world . . .

I felt delighted, and muttered the words to the silent snows around me, listening to the odd acoustics of the cave. I chuckled to myself, and began again when I could remember no further. I forgot how frightening it had all sounded in the dream as I became more adventurous and bellowed the words out in my best Laurence Olivier voice, all the time lying flat on my back in my sleeping bag with my nose protruding from the hood:

> . . . or to be worse than worst
> Of those that lawless and incertain thought
> Imagine howling: – 'tis too horrible!
> The weariest and most loathed worldly life
> That age, ache, penury and imprisonment
> Can lay on nature is a paradise
> To what we fear of death.

When at last I tired of the game, the silence was overwhelming. My boisterous mood vanished and I felt despairingly lonely and silly. I thought of what the words meant, and of the dream, and was close to tears.

My feet had been buried by drifting snow and I yelled at the burning stabs in my knee when I tried to kick them free. While I struggled to roll the wet clinging sleeping bag back over my lower legs I accidently broke a hole in the cave roof. Bright sunshine suddenly burnt away the snow shadows in the cave and I knew at once that the storm was over. I reached for my axe and swept away the rest of the roof. It was going to be a hot day. The sun rapidly melted away the cold night shivers, and I sat in the hole that was left of the cave gazing around me. At my feet, a slope ran down to an old snow-filled crevasse. I was facing the moraines but I couldn't see them from the glacier. Everything was white and alarmingly smooth. The storm had made a good job of covering the footprints I had been following the previous night. For as far as I could see, the surface of the glacier undulated away in unblemished waves of fresh snow.

As I slowly packed the bag into my sack and fumbled to roll up my Karrimat with numb fingers, I realised how desperately thirsty I was. If it had been bad yesterday I couldn't imagine what it would be like today. I tried to think where the nearest flowing water might be. I could remember seeing water only at Bomb Alley, and that was miles away. I would be lucky to reach it today. As soon as the thought struck me I was shocked to see how planned everything had become. I couldn't remember consciously deciding how long it would take to get to camp, yet there was no doubt that I had done so for I had already dismissed any hope of reaching Bomb Alley. Strange things seemed to be going on in my head. I had no clear memory of the sequence of events on the previous day. Vague snatches of unconnected memories came to me – the hollow floor in the crevasse and the sunbeam, an avalanche blast in the storm, falling down the slope where I snow-holed, and that obscene ice cliff – but where had the rest of the day gone. Was this due to lack of food and water? How many days had I been without them? Three days, no, two days and three nights! God Almighty! The thought appalled me. I knew that at this height I needed to consume at least one and a half litres of fluid each day, just to combat the dehydration of altitude. I was running on empty. Food did not worry me. I wasn't hungry, and although I must have burnt up a huge amount of energy, I still felt that I had reserves. But the way my tongue felt thick and coated and kept sticking to my palate frightened me. The smell of water in the sun-heated snow surrounding me drove me close to panic. Eating snow quenched the dryness in my mouth for a short time but I dared not think what was happening inside. It just wasn't possible to eat enough snow to stave off that urgent need for liquid. Whatever planning I had done subconsciously seemed pretty futile as I looked at the snow rolling into the distance. I wasn't going to make it.

Jesus! Is that how it's going to be? Just crawling to a standstill for the sake of water . . .

I slid down the slope and began to crawl away from the snow cave. I thought that I would try to reach the moraines by midday and see how things looked then. Sitting on the glacier feeling worried wasn't going to get me very far. Perhaps I wouldn't make it, maybe I would. I didn't care that much, so long as I kept moving and occupied. It was frightening and lonely to wait for it to come to me.

I crawled carefully. Since there were no tracks to follow, it was vital to try and keep my bearings. I knew that the crevasses were wide and numerous over to my left, so I hugged the right bank of the glacier which curved round beneath Yerupaja. Every now and then I hopped unsteadily on to my good foot to look ahead. The increased view never failed to surprise me. I could see far enough ahead to make out distinctive crevasses which I remembered from our outward trek. However, the nagging fear of unexpected crevasses wore me down, and I became increasingly conscious of how vulnerable I was while crawling.

After an hour I convinced myself that I might be able to walk. My leg, sliding smoothly along behind me, seemed less painful. It occurred to me that I might only have torn some muscles in my knee, and now, after a night's rest, and it being so long since I had hurt it, perhaps it had got sufficiently better to take my weight. I stood up and swayed on my good leg, letting my right foot lie gently on the snow. I pressed down slowly. There was some pain but nothing I couldn't bear. I knew it would hurt but with a bit of determination I reckoned I could keep walking through it. I braced myself and stepped forward on to my right leg. There was a twisting slip inside the joint and bones grated sickeningly.

I lay face-down in the snow, unsure whether I had passed

156

out or not. Nausea threatened to swamp up my throat, making me gasp and retch. Agony boiled from my knee, and I sobbed and cursed at my stupidity. It felt as if I had broken it all over again. The cold bite of the snow on my face cleared the dizziness. I sat up and ate some snow to wash away the bitter sting of bile in my mouth, and then sat slumped forward. When I had stood up, the first series of crevasses running down to the moraines had been visible 100 yards ahead. As I couldn't walk, I would be forced to crawl through the broken section, unable to see far enough ahead to be sure of taking the correct line. Now that I considered it I wasn't certain of the line anyway. I remembered that we had weaved a complex path across the 150 yards of parallel crevasses between me and the moraines, sometimes crossing narrow bridges dividing crevasses, and frequently climbing short steep slopes to avoid the open holes. I doubted that I would be able to control a crawling descent of these obstacles.

I lay back on my rucksack and stared at the sky. My instinct screamed out against attempting the crossing, but my brain could find no alternatives. I ate snow mechanically and drifted into daydreams, abdicating from the inevitable decision to move. There were no clouds to look at, no birds flying by, yet I still lay there, eyes open but unseeing, and thought of anything but where I was.

I awoke with a start – '*Get moving . . . don't lie there . . . stop dozing . . . move!*' The *voice* came through the wandering idle thoughts of pop song lyrics, faces from the past, and fantasies of empty value. I set off crawling, trying to force the pace to salve my guilty conscience. I gave no further thought to what the crevasses might hold for me.

With frequent stops to stand and check the route, I slowly entered the crevasse zone. Dips in the smooth snow made me veer anxiously from side to side, and when I turned to look back, my sloughed tracks meandered crazily in loops and zigzags back to the smooth surface on which I had slept. As in a maze, I thought at first that I knew where I was going; at last I realised I was hopelessly lost. The splits in the ice became more contorted and numerous until I stood up and stared at a broken mess of fissures and covered hollows. It was impossible to judge where I was in relation to the vague map in my mind. I would recognise a crevasse, then look again and see that I was mistaken. Each one changed shape when I glanced at it a second time, and my head was swimming with the effort of concentration. A mounting horror of falling into a crevasse forced me into frantic guessing at the best path through the maze. The harder I tried, the worse my position became, until hysteria threatened to overwhelm me. Which way, which way? Over there . . . and there I would crawl only to find myself dead-ended by another menacing fissure.

Time seemed to slow as I crawled back and forth. I crossed and recrossed my tracks, forgot what I had already seen until I looked at a taunting gap in front of my face once again. I fought the temptation to jump the smaller crevasses, narrow gaps which normally I would have jumped unhesitatingly, but dared not risk leaping off one leg. Even if I cleared the gap, I might slide uncontrollably into the parallel yawning slit immediately ahead.

In a state of nervous exhaustion I collapsed on a narrow bridge of snow between two crevasses. I lay on my side looking bleakly at the narrowing bridge stretching away from me. There was something familiar about the bridge, yet I couldn't recall what it was. I had collapsed in despair when I saw that the bridge narrowed, convinced that once again I would have to retreat. I had already approached this bridge several times before, but now I thought there was something significant about it. On the previous occasions I hadn't dared attempt to stand on the narrow strip of snow for fear of the open holes on either side. I sat up and searched intently for some remembered landmark in the snows ahead. The bridge appeared to curl to the left and drop away. I would be certain that the building excitement within me was justified only if I stood up. Using my axe, I tentatively straightened up, swaying alarmingly and feeling very unsteady.

Beyond the bridge I saw the dark outline of a boulder on a flat snow slope. It was the beginning of the moraines. I dropped back to the bridge and crawled carefully to its narrowest point. The curl to the left led to the snow-covered moraines. There were no more crevasses.

I sat with my back against a large yellow rock, staring at my tracks coming down off the glacier. They weaved crazily through the broken ice as if some giant bird had been hopping around feeding on the snow. I felt utterly drained. It suddenly struck me as funny that I should have taken such a daft route through the crevasses now that I could see clearly the obvious line.

There was a taint of hysteria in my good humour, and the waves of weak shivers running through me left me in no doubt that I had been very lucky to get safely across. The glacier shimmered and waved before my eyes so that its gentle rolls seemed to move like the ocean. I rubbed my eyes and looked again. There was a blurred quality to the view before me, and when I turned to look at the dark moraines tumbling towards the lakes, I noticed that these too appeared hazy and out of focus. The more I rubbed my eyes the worse the blurring became, and sharp prickling burns made tears cloud my sight. Snow-blind!

'Oh shit! That's the last thing I need!'

My sunglasses had smashed when I had fallen from the cliff and broken my leg, and I had been unable to take out my contact lenses for the last two days and nights. I squinted my eyes tight and peered through the smallest of slits. When I looked at the blinding glare of the glacier my eyes burned unbearably and fat tears rolled down my cheeks. The dark moraines were softer, and I found that I could focus quite well there through slitted eyelids. I moved awkwardly to the other side of the boulder, facing the moraines, and that small distance of hopping confirmed my dread that the glacier was the easy part.

I lolled against the rock, feeling luxuriously warm and relaxed in the sun. I promised myself a good rest before attempting the moraines and immediately nodded into sleep. After half an hour the *voice* rudely disturbed my peace, coming into my dreams like the distant murmur of flowing water, with the same insistent message I had so far been unable to ignore:

159

'*Come on, wake up! Things to be done . . . long way to go . . . don't sleep . . . come on.*'

I sat up and stared in confusion at the dark river of rock flowing away from me. For a moment I felt disorientated and wondered where I was.

All those rocks! They were strange after so many days on snow. I hadn't seen so much rock since before the summit. How long ago was that? It took several bemused attempts before I worked it out. Four days ago! It meant nothing to me. Four days, six, what did it matter? Nothing ever seemed to change. I had been in these mountains so long I felt as if I must remain here in this half dream state, waking occasionally in stark reality to remember the reasons for being here, before drifting back to the comfort of fantasy. Rocks! The moraines. Of course! I lay back against the boulder and closed my eyes, but the *voice* kept calling. Instructions tumbled in, repeated commands of what I must do, and I lay back listening and fighting the instinct to obey. I just wanted to sleep a little longer. I lost the fight and obeyed.

The melody of a song continued to play in my head as I organised myself. I found that I could vocalise all the lyrics word-perfectly, yet I was sure I had only been able to remember the refrain in the past. I mumbled it as I draped my sodden sleeping bag over the boulder, and felt content that it must be a good sign. My memory was working fine. I emptied my rucksack on to the snow beside me and sifted through the contents. The small shallow pan and stove were set to one side. I had no gas, so I placed the stove in the stuff sack for my sleeping bag. I took off my helmet and crampons and packed them into the small red bag. My ice hammer and harness just fitted in, and I was left with a torch, camera, sleeping bag, ice axe and pan. I picked the camera from the snow and considered putting it in the bag as well. I had already removed the film after the summit, so it was of no use. I remembered how difficult it had been to find the camera in a secondhand shop and put it into my rucksack. I stuffed my sleeping bag and torch in on top and closed the sack. The shiny aluminium pan was jammed between two small rocks on top of the boulder so that the sun glinted off its surface. I placed the red stuff sack at the base of the boulder and sat back content. It was good to leave things tidy and organised.

The song in my head had changed when I finished, to be replaced by one that I hated. Somehow I couldn't get its insistent chant out of my mind as, irritably, I set to work on my Karrimat, trying to forget the words, . . . *'Brown girl in the ring . . . Tra la la la la . . .'* A part of me performed tasks without conscious decision, as if already told what to do, while the other part insisted on vocalising a stupid meaningless song through my every thought.

I unrolled the yellow foam mat on the snow beside me. It was far too long for what I had in mind. When I tried to tear it in half, I found that the tight closed-cell structure of the mat was too strong. I hacked at it with the adze on my axe, making a crude punctured line across it. When I tore it again it ripped across in a jagged line between the cuts. I wrapped it twice round my knee and pulled it as tight as I could, wincing at the stabs of pain. With a strap from my crampons I buckled it tight on to my upper thigh and struggled with numb fingers to fasten the buckle. Another strap around my calf held it firmly in place. When I lifted my leg I was pleased to see that the knee remained stiff and unbending, but the mat had slipped open at the knee. Two more straps from my rucksack completed the splint. I tightened them very close to the joint, one on either side, and then lay back exhausted. The knee straps had made me yelp when I pulled them tight, but gradually the constant pressure on the knee eased the pain to a throbbing ache.

When I stood up and leant heavily on the boulder, my head spun with giddiness and I gripped the rock harder to stop myself falling. The moment passed. I pulled my sack on to my back and picked my ice axe from the snow. The moraines tumbled away from me in a wide torrent of boulders. I knew that they were very large in the upper reaches of the moraine flow and gradually diminished to rock and scree near the lakes. There was no question of crawling. Walking was also out, so it would have to be hopping.

At the first attempt I fell flat on my face, cracking my forehead sharply on the edge of a boulder, and twisting my knee viciously under me. I screamed. When the pain ebbed, I tried again. I held the axe in my right hand. At less than two feet in length it made a poor walking stick, and I was hunched over like an arthritic pensioner as I placed it carefully on the ground. With all my weight on the axe, I hefted the useless right leg forward so that it hung parallel with my left leg. Bracing myself on the axe I made a violent hop forward. It was too violent, and I swayed precariously, trying to stop myself toppling on to my face again. I had made all of six inches' forward progress! I tried again and fell heavily. The pain took longer to settle, and when I stood again I could feel my knee burning hot beneath the splint.

After covering ten yards I had managed to perfect my hobbling technique. It wasn't very efficient, and I was sweating profusely from the effort. I had worked out that it was best not to place the leg in front of my good foot, and that, rather than making a violent hop, I could execute a swinging step and keep my balance. In those first ten yards I fell at every other hop, but at the end I could hop twice as far and still stay upright. I remembered the patterns I had employed when traversing the ridge and climbing out of the crevasse, and concentrated on the same technique. I broke the hopping down into distinct actions and then repeated them faithfully. Place the axe, lift the foot forward, brace, hop, place the axe, lift-brace-hop, place-lift-brace-hop . . .

I had started down the moraines at one o'clock. Five and a half hours to go before dark. Place-lift-brace-hop. I needed water. I wasn't going to reach Bomb Alley. Place-lift . . . And on until I could hobble automatically and switch myself off. The falls brought me back each time, but they were unavoidable. My axe shaft would slip on a loose rock and send me tumbling half-way through a hop, or I would land on some scree and fall sideways into the boulders. I tried to protect my knee but it was no use. I had no strength in my leg with which to pull it safely to one side. Invariably I fell fully on to it, or bashed it cruelly against the rocky floor. The flares

162

of agony at each impact never diminished but, for some reason, my recovery rate improved dramatically. I stopped screaming when I fell and found that it made no difference. Screaming was for others to hear, and the moraines cared little for my protests. Sometimes I cried, childlike, at the pain and frustration, more often I retched. I was never sick. There was nothing to vomit. When, two hours later, I turned and looked at where I had come from, the glacier was a distant dirty white cliff and my spirits rose at this tangible proof of descent.

The *voice* kept urging me on, '*Place-lift-brace-hop . . . keep going. Look how far you've gone. Just do it, don't think about it . . .*'

I did as I was told. Stumbling past and sometimes over boulders, falling, crying, swearing in a litany that matched the pattern of my hopping. I forgot why I was doing it; forgot even the idea that I probably wouldn't make it. Running on instincts that I had never suspected were in me, and drifting down the sea of moraines in a blurred delirium of thirst, and pain and hopping, I timed myself religiously. I looked ahead to a landmark and gave myself half an hour to reach it. As I neared the mark, a furious bout of watch-glancing would ensue, until it became part of the pattern . . . place-lift-brace-hop-time. If I realised I was behind time I tried to rush the last ten minutes of hopping. I fell so much more when I rushed but it had become so damned important to beat the watch. Only once did I fail to beat it, and I sobbed with annoyance. The watch became as crucial as my good leg. I had no sense of time passing, and with each fall I lay in a semi-stupor, accepting the pain and quite unaware of how long I had been there. A look at the watch would galvanise me into action, especially when I saw it had been five minutes and not the thirty seconds it had felt like.

The boulders dwarfed me. The moraines were as lifeless as the glacier. Drab rock colours all around. Mud, and rocks, and dirty scree. I looked for insects and found none. I saw no birds. It was silent. Outside of the patterns, and the *voice*, my imagination wandered feverishly from one inane thought to another. Songs rustled through my head, and pictures formed in the stones I lay upon. The snow formed in patches between the rocks. It was dirty and full of grit but I ate it continually. Water became an obsession. Pain and water. That was my world. There was nothing else.

I heard water trickling between the rocks. How many times had I heard it trickling? I lay on my chest after the fall, and there was the sound of running water. I inched sideways and the noise increased. I felt myself smiling wolfishly – 'This will be a big one.' I had said it every time, but they were always thin trickles melting into the mud. I moved again towards a crumbling boulder on my right. There! – Ha ha! Told you! – A thin line of silver threaded by the side of the boulder. Bootlace-thin, but bigger than the others. I shuffled nearer on my stomach and peered at the water intently. I had to think about this one.

'Don't touch it! It may sink down again.'

I poked my finger into the gritty mud and the water pooled into the finger hole and flowed on.

'Ah! Got ya!'

The hole was ever so carefully widened until a shallow hollow, the size of a saucer, glistened with water. I bent over it until my nose tickled the surface and then sucked greedily through pursed lips. Half a mouthful of gritty water. I swilled it round, feeling it unstick my palate. I thought that if I swilled it instead of gulping it down I would absorb the water better. It was a daft idea, but I did it nevertheless. The saucer filled slowly. I sucked at it when it was half full and took in too much grit and mud. It caught in my throat and I coughed explosively, spitting the precious fluid back at the pool and destroying the saucer.

I rebuilt the pool but it wouldn't fill. I dug a deeper hole and still it remained dry. It had sunk away. I didn't question where it might have gone. There was no more water until next time. The *voice* interrupted me, and I stood up shakily.

The afternoon stayed clear. There wouldn't be a storm in the night. The sky would stay clear and starry, and it would be cold without the clouds. I looked ahead for a landmark and saw the moraines fall in a steep drop fifty feet away. I recognised it immediately. This was where the ice beneath the moraines stood out in a steep cliff. We had left Richard after passing these cliffs when we had come up before. I was hugging the right bank of the moraines where the boulders were least chaotic, and here the steep water-smoothed rocky sides pinched down on the moraines to form the cliffs. Eighty-foot-high mud-covered glassy smooth ice. I remembered now. We had climbed a twisting path up them, carefully avoiding the many large rocks that had been left in precarious balance as the sun melted the ice away. I felt strangely excited to have reached the cliffs. They were the last obstacle which could kill me. Once past the cliffs I had only to keep crawling. There would be no more crevasses or cliffs to threaten me. I timed myself and hobbled towards the top of the cliffs.

I sat at the start of the path down the cliff, trying to assess the best method of descent. Should I sit facing outwards and shuffle down on my bum, or lie on my stomach and lower myself with my axe? I regretted having left my crampons behind. One crampon would have made all the difference. I decided to face out, sitting on my bum. At least that way I could always see where I was going.

Half-way down the cliff I began to feel cocky. It had been so easy. What had I been so scared about? The answer came abruptly as the rock I was holding came unstuck and I jerked sideways and started sliding. I clawed at the muddy ice, trying to grab at the rocks embedded in it. I rolled over and pressed my chin against the ice, bumping my head repeatedly, desperate to slow the slide. Suddenly I stopped. My left boot had jammed against an edge of rock. I shook violently.

A couple of times I looked back at the ice cliffs as I hobbled away down the rocks. Each time they grew smaller and I felt that I was shutting the door on something intangible but menacing that had been with me for so long. Those cliffs were the doors to the mountains. I grinned when I glanced at them. I had won a battle of some sort. I could feel it deep inside. Now it was just the patterns, and the pain, and water. Could I reach Bomb Alley tonight? Now that would be something to grin about! It wasn't so far from here, twenty minutes' walk, and that couldn't be so hard!

And that was my mistake. I stopped timing landmarks and set my sights on Bomb Alley and the silver floods of icy melt-water pouring down its flanks. When it became dark I had no idea how far Bomb Alley was, nor did I know how far I had crawled. Without checking my watch I had lain in stupefied exhaustion after every fall. Lain there and listened to endless stories running through the pain, watched short dreams of life in the real world, played songs to my heartbeat, licked the mud for water, and wasted countless hours in an empty dream. Now I staggered blind in the dark, obsessed with Bomb Alley, ignoring the *voice* which told me to sleep, and rest, and forget the alley. I got my head-torch from my sack and blundered on until the light died. It was a moonless night. The stars threw bright patterns across the sky, glimmering faint light on to the moraines.

At ten o'clock I tripped and fell heavily on to the rocks. I had fallen on almost every hop since the torch had failed three hours earlier, and I knew in the back of my mind that I had made only a few hundred yards in all that time. Now, I couldn't stand up. I tried, but somehow I couldn't make enough effort to raise myself. There was an over-ride stopping me. The *voice* prevailed. I shuffled into my sleeping bag and immediately fell asleep.

12

TIME RUNNING OUT

I flung my sleeping bag across the tent roof and walked over to the shade of the cooking rock. The deep tiredness I had felt yesterday was gone. Indeed the only remaining evidence of my ordeal was the sight of my blackened fingertips. Already I was forgetting that they were damaged and was surprised when I couldn't fiddle with the small key to the petrol stove. Richard took it from me and lit the stove. He was quiet as he prepared breakfast. I sensed what was on his mind but chose not to talk about it. Last night he had broached the subject of returning to Lima. There was nothing to keep us at camp, and he had to renew his visa within the next five days. I told him that I still needed to rest and recover. It might have been true last night, but not now. I was fully recovered. My voracious appetite attested to it, and Richard must have noticed the improvement.

The bitter feelings, however, hadn't diminished. To leave the place would free me from an unrelenting presence which accused me, and the chaotic bustle of Lima would erase the silence which seemed to bear down on me each time I was alone in camp. In my heart I knew I should go but I couldn't make the break. The mountains held me in thrall. Something prevented me from leaving. I wasn't afraid to return and face the music. I had done the right thing; no one could challenge my conviction that I was as much a victim as Joe. It wasn't a crime to have survived. So why not go? I gazed across at the icy white sweep of Sarapo. Perhaps tomorrow . . .

'Feeling better?' *Richard interrupted my thoughts.*

'Yes. Yes, much better. It's only the fingers now . . .' I trailed off and stared at my fingers, anxious to avoid his eyes.

'I think we should leave.'

I had expected him to take his time. His blunt statement shocked me.

'What? . . . Yes. I suppose you're right. It's just . . . I'm not ready. I . . .'

'Staying isn't going to help. Is it?'

'No, probably not.' I peered more closely at my hands.

'Well then, I think we should see about organising the donkeys. Spinoza is down at the huts. I can go down and sort it out with him.'

I said nothing. Why did I feel so strongly against moving? There was nothing to gain. To stay was stupid. Why . . . ?

'Look,' Richard said softly, 'he's not coming back. You know it. If there was a chance you'd have gone back up yesterday. Right? So leave it. There's a lot to do. We have to inform the Embassy, and his folks, and go through all the legal hassle and get flights booked, and all that. I think we should go.'

'Perhaps you could go on ahead. I can follow later. You go tell the Embassy and stuff, and get your visa. I'll follow in a few days.'

'Why? Come down with me. It'll be better that way.'

I didn't answer, and he stood up and went to his tent. He came out with his money belt.

'I'm going down to see Spinoza. I'll try to persuade him to come with the donkeys sometime today. We can get to Huayallapa if we leave at midday. If he can't manage it I'll get him to come early tomorrow morning.'

He turned and set off for the huts at the foot of the valley. As he began to cross the river bed I got up and ran after him:

'Hey, Richard!' He turned to face me. 'You're right,' I shouted. 'Get Spinoza to bring the donkeys tomorrow, not today. We'll go first thing in the morning. Okay?'

'Yeah, okay. See you soon.'

He turned and walked briskly across the dry river bed. I had the tea ready when, two hours later, I saw him returning.

He gave me some cheese which he had bought from the girls, and we sat on our Karrimats to eat it in the sun.

'He'll be here at six in the morning,' he said, 'but you know what their idea of time is like.'

'Good.'

I felt happy now that the decision had been made. The weight of brooding lifted from me at the prospect of things to do, and there was much to be done. We had a two-day walk ahead of us. The camp needed to be dismantled and packed into loads of equal weight. How many kilos to a donkey was it? Two loads of twenty on each side? Doesn't matter. We'll have half the weight going down. We'll have to pay Spinoza as well. Perhaps we could negotiate some barter. There are lots of things here that he would want; ropes, pans, penknives. Yeah, we can make some bargain out of them. Then we have to book on the bus at Cajatambo, and tell the police we're returning to Lima. Now that's a problem! They will want to know about Joe. Don't tell them. It'll avoid a lot of stress. We can do all that in Lima, and the Embassy will be there to help us. I'll have to ring Joe's parents. Oh God! What am I going to say? Just tell them he died in a crevasse, and give them the whole story when you get back. Yes, that would be best. I hope we get an early flight back. I don't fancy hanging around Lima for very long. I won't see Bolivia now. Joe wanted to go to Ecuador, and I wanted to see Bolivia. Ironic that we won't see either of them.

'Hey.' I looked up to see Richard bending over a boulder behind the dome tent.

'What?'

'Didn't you hide your money before going to Siula?'

'Jesus! I forgot about that.' I got up and hurried over to where he was standing. 'It's not there. I hid it under a rock near the gas store.'

We searched near the store but couldn't find it. I racked my brains to remember exactly where I had put the small plastic bag with 200 dollars wrapped inside.

'Perhaps it's over there,' I muttered dubiously. Richard burst out laughing.

'This is great! If we don't find it we're going to have trouble getting back to Lima. Come on, surely you remember the place?'

'Yeah, well, I thought I did, but I'm not sure. It was a week ago!'

As I said it I recognised a rock at the back of the gas store, and when I lifted it there lay the bag of money.

'Got it!' I shouted triumphantly, holding the bag above my head.

Richard bobbed up from behind a boulder.

'Thank God for that! I was just beginning to think that the kids might have found it.'

He then started preparing a meal while I counted the bills to see how much I had left: 195 dollars. It was enough. I wondered how long we would have to stay in the city sorting things out with the Embassy and the police. There was bound to be a lot of bureaucratic time-wasting.

'What about Joe's money?' I said abruptly, and Richard stopped stirring the pan.

'What money?'

'Well, he hid his stash as well, remember?'

'He never told me about it.'

'He certainly told me. In fact he was quite adamant about it. He dragged me over to show me exactly where he was hiding it.'

'Go and get it then.'

'I can't. I've forgotten the place.'

Richard guffawed loudly. I laughed too and wondered at myself. The spontaneous humour of the last hour surprised me – and the way I had said 'Joe's money' without once feeling it had anything to do with him. I had burnt his ghost yesterday. The money was simply money, not his. Ours, if we could only find it.

'How much did he have?'

'Quite a bit. More than me, anyway.'

'Well, we'd better find it then. I'm not leaving 200-plus dollars to rot under a rock.'

He stood up and walked over to the gas store and began

peering under the surrounding boulders. It was my turn to cackle uproariously.

'What the hell are you doing? You haven't a clue where he hid it, and there're thousands of bloody rocks round here.'

'Got any better suggestions? You were the one who forgot the hiding place.'

'We'll do it systematically. It's certainly nowhere near the gas store, that's for sure!'

I walked to an area of large boulders and tried to find one that would jog my memory. They all looked the same to me. I quartered the area until I was satisfied the money wasn't there, and then moved to another group of boulders. Richard stood quietly to one side grinning knowingly. After an hour's fruitless searching I stopped and looked at him.

'Come on then. Don't just stand there. Help me.'

An hour later we sat morosely by the stove drinking tea. We hadn't found the money.

'It's got to be there somewhere, for Christ's sake! I know he put it under a small stone near a boulder, and it was no more than ten yards from the dome tent.'

'As you said, there're thousands of rocks here.'

Between bouts of argumentative tea-drinking, the search continued without result. At four o'clock the two girls appeared in camp with two of the children. We stopped searching and pretended that we were organising the camp site. They smiled sadly at me, and I found them unnerving. Richard had told them of Joe's death when he had gone down to arrange the donkeys with Spinoza. The carefree sunny afternoon suddenly seemed to cloud over as I looked at their show of grief. They angered me. What right had they to feel sad? I had been through all that, and didn't like to be reminded.

Richard made some tea for them as they squatted near the stove looking at me with the same open and unabashed curiosity as they had when we first met. It felt as if they were examining me for signs of strain. I took their silence for pity. The two children stared at me open-mouthed. I wondered if they expected me suddenly to do something spectacular. The

171

elder girl spoke briefly to Richard. I didn't understand what she said, but saw his face darken with anger.

'They want to know what we are going to give them!' He said it incredulously.

'What?'

'That's all. Nothing about Joe. They don't give a toss!'

The girls were chattering to each other as we spoke, occasionally smiling expectantly at one or other of us. When Norma reached over and began sorting through the cooking utensils I exploded. I jumped up, waving my arms. Norma dropped the frying pan and looked at Gloria in alarm.

'Go away! Go on! Vayase. Go on. PISS OFF!'

They sat stock-still in bewilderment. They didn't seem to understand and appeared confused.

'Come on, Richard. You tell them, and quick, before I hit one of them.'

I spun round and stormed away from the tents. Minutes later I saw the girls helping the children on to their mules, and riding off down the valley. I was shaking with fury when I returned.

As darkness fell the first heavy spots of rain pattered on to the tents. We retreated to the dome and cooked the evening meal on gas stoves in the entrance. The rain turned to heavy wet snowflakes, and we zipped the tent closed. Tomorrow the donkeys would arrive and we could leave this place. I felt relieved. At about seven o'clock an eerie sound wailed out from the cloud-filled valley.

'What the hell was that?'

'Dogs.'

'Bloody odd-sounding dog!'

'You'd be surprised. When you were on the mountain I heard the weirdest things at night. Used to scare the tripes out of me.'

We finished a game of gin rummy, blew out the candle and settled down. I thought of the snow falling on the glacier beneath Siula and the hollow ache hurt with a vengeance.

I opened my eyes and flinched at the sharp glare of sunlight.

Tears brimmed and watered my vision. I closed my eyes and made a mental check on myself. Cold and weak. It was still early and the sun had no warmth. Sharp stones pressed through the sodden fabric of my sleeping bag. My neck ached. I had slept with my head crooked over between two rocks. The night had taken forever to pass. There had been little sleep. The hammering falls had severely affected my leg so that spasms of pain kept disturbing me when I dozed off. Once I had howled in agony when cramps in my thigh and calf muscles forced me to twist violently and bend forward to massage the injured leg. When the pain throbbed too insistently for sleep, I had lain shivering on the rocky cleft where I had collapsed and stared at the night sky. Shooting-stars flared in the myriad bands of stars spread across the night. I watched them flare and die without interest. As the hours passed, the feeling that I would never get up over-whelmed me. I lay unmoving on my back, feeling pinned to the rocks, weighed down by a numb weariness and fear until it seemed that the star-spread blackness above me was pushing me relentlessly into the ground. I spent so much of the night wide-eyed, staring at the timeless vista of stars, that time seemed frozen and spoke volumes to me of solitude and loneliness, leaving me with the inescapable thought that I would never move again. I fancied myself lying there for centuries, waiting for a sun that would never rise. I slept in sudden stolen minutes and awoke to the same stars and the same inevitable thoughts. They talked to me without my consent, whispering dreads that I knew were untrue but couldn't ignore. The *voice* told me I was too late; time had run out.

Now my head was basked in sunshine while my body lay shadowed by a large boulder on my left. I pulled the draw-cord open with my teeth and tried to shuffle out of the bag and into the sun. Every movement caused flares of pain in my knee. Though I moved only six feet, the effort left me slumped in exhaustion on the screes. I could hardly believe how badly I had deteriorated during the night. Pulling myself along with my arms had become the limit of my strength. I shook my head from side to side, trying to wake myself and drive the lethargy away. It had no effect, and I lay back on the rocks. I had hit some sort of wall. I wasn't sure whether it was mental or physical but it smothered me in a blanket of weakness and apathy. I wanted to move but couldn't. Lifting my arm to shield the sun from my eyes required a deliberate struggle. I lay motionless, frightened by my weakness. If I could get water I would have a chance. It would be just one chance. If I didn't reach camp that day then I would never do so.

Will the camp still be there?

The question sprang to mind for the first time, and with it came the dread feelings I had experienced in the night. Perhaps they had gone. Simon must have been back for two days . . . more, this was the morning of his third day! There was no reason for him to stay once he had recovered his strength.

I sat up suddenly without effort. The thought of being left galvanised me from my lethargy. I must reach camp today. I checked my watch. Eight o'clock. I had ten hours of daylight ahead of me.

I hauled myself to my feet, pulling desperately at the boulder, and wavered uncertainly on the verge of collapsing back on to the scree. My head whirled with the sudden change of position, and for a moment I thought I was going to black out. Blood roared in my temples, my legs seemed to liquefy. I hugged the rough rock of the boulder and held on tight. When my balance returned and the roaring eased I straightened up and looked back to where I had come from yesterday. I was disappointed to find that I could still see the top of the ice cliffs in the far distance. Turning towards the lakes I saw that I was a long way above the site of Bomb Alley. All that staggering in the dark had been for nothing. How stupid it had been to forget the watch-keeping yesterday, and how quickly I had lost any idea of time. Bomb Alley had then become a vague aim instead of a carefully planned objective. Without timing each stage I had drifted aimlessly with no sense of urgency. Today it had to be different. I decided that four hours would be enough to reach Bomb Alley. Twelve

Simon reaching Siula Grande's spectacularly unsafe summit. (Photo: Simpson)

Below: Joe, looking exhausted at the summit on 8th June 1985. (Photo: Yates)

Over page: Cold and frostbitten, Simon rests in the fragile snow cave on the North Ridge below the summit, from which the photograph of Yerupaja bathed in morning light was taken. (Photo: Simpson)

Joe and Simon leave their tracks on the North Ridge – shortly before all interest in photography ended. (Photo: Yates)

The storm-shrouded face down which Simon tried to rescue Joe by lowering him again and again on 300 feet of rope. (Photo: Simpson)

The ice cliffs – a tricky proposition with a broken leg. (Photo: Simpson)

Two views of the river of moraines below the glacier *(below and opposite)*, Siula Grande above, Yerupaja to the right. Joe's route back to camp is shown in the map on pages 12 and 13. (Photos: Simpson and Yates)

Simon, believing Joe to have died in the crevasse, nurses a harrowing guilt in camp while Joe crawls through the mud and silent screes back to base. *Right:* Joe lies unconscious at Simon's feet while Spinoza and the girls strike camp. (Photos: Richard Hawking)

Richard (left) walks beside Joe (on the donkey) at the start of the two-day walk to Cajatambo. (Photo: Yates)

Joe, exhausted, resting during the second day's agonising mule journey. (Photo: Hawking)

noon was the deadline, and I intended to break those hours into short stages, each one carefully timed. I searched ahead for the first landmark – a tall pillar of red rock that stood out clearly above the sea of boulders. Half an hour to reach it, and then I would look for another.

I hoisted my sack on to my back and crouched to make the first tentative hop of the day. The moment I jumped I knew I would fall. My arm buckled and I pitched forward. When I tried to stand for another try I couldn't raise myself on the axe. Once again I hugged the boulder and clawed myself upright. Fifteen minutes later I was still within sight of where I had slept. I swayed unsteadily as I looked back at my progress. At every hop I fell, but it was the attempt at standing that demoralised me. The first fall had been abominably painful and I had lain face-down in the gravel, clenching my teeth, waiting for the pain to subside. It remained with me, burning my knee unbearably as it had never done before.

'Stop, stop, please stop . . .'

But it stayed. I stood up despite the pain in an attempt to force it into the background. I could feel my facial muscles screwing up and my mouth pulled into a rictus of protest. I fell again. The pain stayed level. Perhaps the knee was so traumatised that it had gone beyond the normal boundaries of pain. Perhaps it was in my head.

In those fifteen minutes I lost whatever fight was left in me. I felt it ebb out of me with every fall as the chronic burning pain took over. I stood and fell, writhed where I fell, cried and swore, and felt sure in my heart that these were my last spastic efforts before I lay still for good. I let go my grip on the boulder and tried to hop. My foot didn't leave the ground, and I toppled sideways unable even to protect myself with my arms.

The blow stunned me. For a while pain disappeared as my head swam in sick dizziness half-way between consciousness and oblivion. I had cut my lip on the rock and tasted the blood trickling into my mouth. I lay crumpled on my side between two large boulders. The red pillar stood out from the moraines directly in front of me. I checked my watch. Ten minutes left to reach it. No chance! I closed my eyes and laid my cheek against the cool rocky ground. Through a hazy blur I thought of how far I had to go, and of how far I had come. Part of me cried out to give up and sleep, and accept that I would never reach camp. The *voice* countered this. I lay still and listened to the argument. I didn't care about the camp or getting down. It was too far. Yet the irony of collapsing on the moraines after having overcome all those obstacles angered me. The *voice* won. My mind was set. It had been from the moment I got out of the crevasse.

I would keep moving, keep trying, for want of other choices. After Bomb Alley I would aim for the upper lake, then cross the intervening moraines to the lower lake, contour round the lake to the moraines at its end, and after climbing them descend to camp. At least, I told myself that this would happen. I no longer cared whether it did or not.

I hopped forward to the lip of a hollow, fell, and rolled sideways into it. I heard water splashing over slabs from a long grey distance in my head. My face was wet. The muddy gravel at the base of the water-smooth rock was cold and moist. When I turned to face the sound, I saw a silver sheen of melt-water pouring over the golden rock. I had reached Bomb Alley. It was one o'clock. I was an hour overdue.

A great rounded wall of rock curved above the hollow in which I lay. The floor of the hollow was sodden. A cone of muddy scree was piled at the base of the rock, rising to a stream of water pouring down the slab. The sun shone fully on to the rock, melting the snow above it. With a strength I hadn't possessed minutes before, I scrambled over to the cone of scree and with one sweep of my axe brushed it aside. I pressed my lips to the thin trickle. It was icy cold. I gasped for breath between frantic sucks at the wet slab. Water splashed over my forehead, running over my closed eyes and off the tip of my nose. I snorted, pig-like, as a gasp for air sucked the water up my nostrils, then I pushed my face back to the rock.

A long time passed before I calmed my assault on the trickle. By then the terrible dry burning in my throat had been soothed, but the thirst remained. With every mouthful I could feel my strength returning. I sat side-on to the rock and my polar trousers sopped up the water from the wet screes. When sense at last prevailed, I scooped a hollow from the debris at the scree cone and watched it fill. Two inches of icy clear water filled the scoop – more than I could take in one mouthful. The hollows refilled before I could bend again for a second drink. I drank until my stomach hurt with the cold weight of water, and then drank more. I bent my face to the pool and slobbered at the water, coughing as grit caught in my throat, and trying to drink at the same time. I heard myself mewling and groaning with the delight and discomfort.

Each time I stopped, thinking I had drunk my fill, an overpowering urge to drink again would come over me. Mud and grit smeared my face and I clawed at the pool, enlarging it with numb, soiled fingers. I drank, rested, and drank again with the panicky obsession that it might suddenly dry up and disappear. Three days and nights without water had maddened me. I couldn't tear myself away from the rock, and drank with eyes tight-closed and face clenched in unbelieving astonishment. More water than I had ever dared think of, enough to fill the blotting paper feeling within me and turn me away, sodden and sponged, to collapse sated on the floor of the hollow.

I roused myself from the stupor of fluid and looked around. Sounds of water tinkling near me were a comfort. The hollow felt familiar. I had been here with Simon and Richard, and then a second time with Simon. How long ago? Eight days ago! It seemed unbelievable. I remembered the place so well that it seemed only yesterday that we had sat here on our rucksacks, filled with excitement about the climb. A few small stones rattled down the water rock. I ducked away instinctively as they smacked into the screes at the far end of the hollow. The water had wrought an amazing change in me. I felt invigorated. The previous hours of despair were forgotten. The empty soft weakness I had felt since waking had gone. I could feel my fight returning. The wall I had stumbled through that morning had been washed away.

From Bomb Alley I knew that the upper lake was half an

hour's walking, or three hours' crawling. I decided to try and reach it by four o'clock. I stood up and hopped to the rock for one last drink, then turned and began to leave the hollow. As I reached its far end I saw footprints in the mud. I stopped and stared at them. I recognised the print of Simon's boots, and the smaller marks of Richard's trainers. My spirits rose. They were with me. I hopped past.

The moraines ahead of me were less chaotic. The mass of huge boulders tossed at random over the upper reaches gave way to smaller stones spread in a carpet between occasional erratic boulders. They shifted and slipped under my axe. I fell, but not against boulders, and now I could stand with less effort. The water had revived me but the sun, burning mercilessly from a clear sky, sapped my concentration. I found myself drifting dazedly in and out of sleep, waking with a jerk, and sitting up from the fall, shaking the sleep from my head.

The patterns happened of their own accord. I gave them no thought. They were as natural as walking. The *voice* still urged me on but without the insistent commanding tone of yesterday. Now it seemed to suggest that I might as well get on with it for want of anything else to do. I found it easier to ignore it and slump on the ground in a sleepy daydream. Yeah, sure, I'll move, but I'll rest a little longer first . . . and the *voice* would fade into a background of hazy dreams. Conversations from the past, in voices I recognised immediately, competing with incessant tunes and mental pictures of remembered places, drifted in and out of my mind like a crazy disjointed Sixties film. I swayed drunkenly on every rock large enough to lean against and let the sleep whisk me away from the endless landscape of dull dirty rocks.

Only my watch kept me in touch with the day. The hours passed unnoticed. I remembered the minutes of each dreamy rest and no more. When I fell on to my leg, the pain flared and I cried or groaned until it faded, then dreamed. It felt so normal to hurt that I was no longer surprised by the torment which ambushed me with every fall. Sometimes I wondered dully why it didn't hurt when I had fallen heavily. I asked myself endless questions, none of which I answered; but not once did I question what was happening. Muttered arguments jolted me awake, and I wondered who I had been talking to; many times I looked behind me to see who they were, but they were never there. I hobbled down a path I knew instinctively. I paid no heed to the landscape around me. The ground I covered was forgotten the minute I had passed it. Behind me lay a hazy memory of falls and boulders jumbled into a timeless idea of what I had so far done. Ahead lay more of the same.

At three o'clock I reached a point where the rocks funnelled into a steep gully. It cut down deeply, bearing a muddy yellow clay. A stream twisted along its base. This was the end of the moraines proper. I knew that the gully ran all the way to the lake, widening as it descended until it cut a flat clay-based path out from the snout of the moraines. I couldn't hop down it, so I sat with my legs in front of me and shuffled down the clay. The walls of the gully rose high above me and boulders hung over the sides in precarious balance. It was shadowed and cool in there. Occasionally I lay on my back and looked at the gully walls framing the sky above me and muttered vaguely remembered songs. The water seeped through my clothes, and when I sat up I felt it trickle down my back and soak into my sodden trousers. If I felt like it, I rolled on to my side and sucked noisily at the filthy water running down the gully bed. Mostly I shuffled down lost in a different world.

I stared ahead at the gradually widening yellow gully and peopled it with other figures shuffling along its bed. I imagined an exodus of cripples taking this yellow path to the sea, then thought of food, and the vision disintegrated. Every now and then I saw a boot print and wondered idly whose it was, until I remembered Simon and Richard at Bomb Alley and knew for certain that they followed close behind me. I smiled, happy at the thought of company and help if I needed it. They would come if I called, but I wasn't going to call. They hung back out of sight, but I knew they weren't far behind. They're embarrassed by my condition, I told myself, and felt ashamed. All that water had made me want to pee but

I hadn't managed to remove my clothing in time. I was sure they would understand. So I went on until the bubble abruptly burst and their comforting presence vanished.

I stopped dead, shocked at my sudden return to reality, feeling scared. Before long another song played through the fear and, looking ahead, I saw the sunshine glimmering off the surface of the lake. I grinned at the sight and increased my speed.

'Four o'clock and all's well,' I shouted at the lake, and laughed foolishly.

A flat gravel plain ran out from the gully, forming a crescent-shaped beach at the lakeside. I tried to stand now that I had no downward pull to help me shuffle. When I stood shakily on one foot the lake swam before my eyes and blood pounded from my head. I hit the gravel with a sickening crash and heard, as if from a long way off, a cry of pain. I tried again, but fell before I could stand. My leg had gone to jelly.

At first I decided it was because I had been shuffling for so long, then I realised that I was too weak to hop any more. I grimaced at the fiery wet rush of urine flooding down my thigh, and when it stopped and began to cool I tried once again to stand. The best I could manage was an arthritic bent-over crouch, with the axe shaft wobbling under my weight. I swung my bad leg forward and seemed to topple over for no reason. I hadn't the strength even to stand still. I resorted to a forward belly-crawl.

The water of the lake was astonishingly clear. Coppered green shadows glinted in its depths. Ice cliffs on the far shore overhung the water in hulking dirty grey mounds. A waterfall splashed noisily over the ice, and an occasional breeze ruffled the water so that it seemed to dance dappled silver and green reflections towards me. I lay on my chest with my head hanging over the small rocky drop to the water in front of me. I had slept, woken to stare at the lake, and slept again. The sun dried the gully water from my trousers. There was a warm stench of urine which drifted around me on the light airs. One hour I had slept, and now I looked across the lake wondering whether I should try standing again.

The lake stretched towards base camp in a long narrow ribbon. In the distance I could see where a jumble of moraines cut the lake in half. I knew that beyond those moraines the second smaller circular lake pooled against the dam of moraines above the tents. Except for the short passage through the moraines the ground was generally flat. The beach-like gravel extended to the moraine dam, and beyond the dam it was all downhill. It would be easy ground over which to hop, if only I could stand. It would be much faster to hop. If I reached the top of the dam before dark I would be able to look down on the tents – if they were still there. They might hear me if I shouted, and rush up to me. If they had left . . .

I looked back at the water. If they had gone, what then? The prospect terrified me. I knew the answer only too well. I couldn't believe that they would have left. It seemed inconceivable after my efforts. Nothing could be that cruel? Surely I had left such malevolence behind when I had climbed down the ice cliffs and passed the door to the mountains? A part of me hesitated, paralysing any thought of moving. I didn't want to get there before dark. It would destroy me if I saw that the tents had gone.

The *voice* said, '*Don't be a fool, hurry on; two hours' light left.*'

I stared into the lake, caught between too many fears, unable to act. When I stood up it seemed that I lifted a heavy weight with me, an almost solid feeling of dread that had crept through me, and I despaired of going any further. I managed two hops before falling heavily. I crawled forward on my stomach. My foot dragged over the gravel, jolting my knee. I sat up, faced the way I had come, and shuffled along backwards, as I had done on the glacier. I moved towards the second lake at a desperately slow pace, but I didn't stop, and gradually I could see that I was getting there. I followed the edge of the lake and the soft lapping sounds of the water murmured continuously as I drifted back into dreamland. I remembered a time of falling, plunging snow-bound down a mountain, and heard the same soft murmur of waves on a shingle beach. I had thought myself dying then, and now the same lapping melody pursued my shuffling progress.

The lake had seemed far longer than it was, and an hour later I had crossed the dividing moraines and started along the bank of the second lake. I recognised the place where I had attempted to fish for trout, and stopped to look ahead at the dam of moraines. It had taken me fifteen minutes to walk to camp from here. I tried to guess how long it would take me to crawl, and became hopelessly confused when I realised it had been a brisk hour's walk from camp to Bomb Alley. It had taken me five hours to descend to the second lake. I found it impossible to grasp how slowly I was moving. Yet, as I looked at the dam, I felt sure I could reach it before dark. I had one hour left.

The sun had been blotted out by a rolling blanket of cumulus clouds coming from the east. They looked dark and swollen as they packed into the valley walls. It was going to storm. I reached the moraine dam just as the first drops of rain spattered down. The wind had increased and gusted cold blasts of ice-cooled air across the lake. I shivered.

The wall of the dam was comprised of compacted mud and gravel. I remembered that I had slipped and fallen when climbing it before. A few rocks jutted out from the mud, which was tilted at an angle of $45°$. At its head, a jagged crown of loose boulders was outlined against lowering storm clouds. Snowflakes whipped past me mixed into the rain. The temperature was dropping rapidly.

I used my axe on the mud as if it were ice, reaching up and hacking the pick into the wall and then hauling myself up with my arms. I kicked my boot into the slope with little effect. I scraped my boot across the slope until it lodged accidently on a small edge of stone jutting from the mud. Another swing of the axe and I had to repeat the whole precarious process while my injured leg hung uselessly beneath me. The higher I climbed, the more nervous I became. I thought it was because I was scared of falling and having to begin again, but it went deeper than that. The dark dread of what I might find at the top was becoming unbearable. It had been with me from the very beginning. In the crevasse it had been overshadowed by terror, on the glacier by loneliness, but once past all the dangers it had mushroomed into a consuming hollowness. Something huge and bloated wallowed in my chest, squeezing my throat and emptying my guts. My nerves jumped and twisted, and every thought in my head was focused on the possibility of finding myself abandoned, not just for a second time, but for good.

At the top of the mud slope I crawled between a jumble of rocks until I had reached the highest point of the moraines. I pulled myself upright and leant against a large boulder. There was nothing to be seen. Clouds filled the valley below and snow flurries eddied back and forth in the wind. If the tents were there I couldn't see them. It was almost dark. I cupped my hands to my mouth and shouted:

'SIIIMMMOONNNN!'

It echoed off the clouds, and the wind whipped it away. I screamed a high-pitched howl at the clouds and heard an eerie echo from the gathering darkness. Had they heard me? Would they come?

I slumped down by the boulder, sheltering from the wind, and waited. The cold ate through me as darkness quickly swamped the clouds from view. I listened intently for the answering call, knowing it would never come, and when I could sit still no longer for the shivering I shuffled away from the boulder. There was a long descent of grass and cactus-covered hillside ahead. I had considered getting my sleeping bag out and resting the night on the moraines but the *voice* said, '*Don't*', and I agreed. It was too cold. To sleep now would be to never wake up. I huddled my shoulders against the wind and, facing forward, shuffled down the hillside.

Hours of darkness drifted by and I lost all sense of place and time. I shuffled in short inching slides, peering round at the surrounding darkness in confusion. The idea that I was descending to the tents had long since evaporated. I had no conception of what I was doing, and knew only that I must keep moving. The wind-blown snow spattered my face in icy gusts. It would wake me from deep timeless sleeps and force the crawl to begin again. Occasionally I glanced at my watch, switching the light on and squinting at the clock face. Nine o'clock, eleven o'clock, the night stretched on, and the five hours' crawling from the moraine dam meant nothing. I vaguely knew it should have taken me only ten minutes to reach the camp. Five hours could have been ten minutes. I no longer understood.

When sharp cactus spines sliced into my thighs I would stop and explore the ground beneath me, quite incapable of understanding what had pierced me. The night blanketed everything from sight, and I slipped into a delirium of muttered words and distorted ideas of where I was and what I was doing. Was I still on the glacier? Better be careful, I thought, the crevasses are bad at the end. And where have all the rocks gone? It was good not to feel thirsty, but I wished I knew where I was . . .

13

TEARS IN THE NIGHT

Almost without noticing it I had entered a wide area of rocks and river gravels. Moraines again? I was unsure. The steep descent of grass and cactus had disorientated me. When I turned to look behind me, a dark sinuous line was just visible on the white snow-covered hillside. There was no snow on the rocks. Which rocks were these? I fumbled in the rucksack until I found my head-torch. A dull yellow glow flared briefly when I turned it on. I shone it round in a circle and saw grey tumbled rocks. I was sitting in a huge barren field of them, quite unable to choose which way to crawl. The torch beam died quickly. I discarded it and moved forward into the darkness with my head whirling in confusion. I tried to think clearly, sweeping away the medley of mad thoughts for brief snatches of reality. The river bed! That was where I was, though the realisation didn't help, for I slept immediately and woke later unable to remember it. The notion that I was on the river bed flitted through my mind but I failed to grasp it again and insisted on returning to wilder ideas.

The river bed was half a mile wide, strewn with rocks and pocked with pools of icy melt-water. Somewhere out in the darkness lay the river. I couldn't hear it for the storm winds. The tents were snuggled on its far bank, but where was I? Was I moving towards the centre or curving back towards the moraine dam? Does anyone care? I kept shuffling along, bumping my feet up against rocks, moaning at the spasms of pain, muttering questions to the darkness and hearing only the sibilant rush of stormy wind in answer. The *voice* had left me hours ago. I was glad not to be bothered by its interruptions.

Instinct made me turn my course from side to side, as if I recognised the jumbled stones, saw familiar patterns in the darkness, and followed a subconscious compass bearing. How far were the tents? Perhaps they're gone! I could wait till morning showed me the way, so I sat waiting in the wind. I found myself moving again, unsure how long I had waited. If I waited it would never come. A watched kettle never boils! What a silly saying. I cackled inanely at my private joke and kept on laughing long after I had forgotten the joke.

When I checked my watch I found that it was morning. Yet another day. A quarter to one in the morning. I felt the rough edge of a large boulder against my shoulder and pulled myself up it until I could sit swaying on its top. Something told me that I was close. I stared through the darkness. It must be here; I could feel it. There was a high, sharp faecal smell gusting round me. I sniffed my mitts, flinching with repugnance at the stench. It took a long time to sink in.

'Shit? . . . Why am I sitting in shit?'

I slumped back on the boulder. I knew where I was but seemed incapable of acting on it. I stared bleakly into the darkness. The cooking rock would be sticking up somewhere ahead of me, but where? Sudden flurries of snow whipped my face and I raised my hand to protect myself. The sharp stench caught in my nostrils, and my head suddenly cleared. All I had to do was shout! I sat up, yelled hoarsely into the darkness. The word came out strangled and distorted. I sat dumbly peering ahead, waiting.

Perhaps they had gone. The cold was taking me again. I felt its insidious touch on my back. I wouldn't survive this night, that was for sure, but I no longer cared. The notions of living or dying had long since become tangled. The past days merged into a blur of real events and madness, and now I seemed fixed in a limbo between the two. Alive, dead, was there that much difference? I raised my head and howled a name into the darkness:

'SIIIIMMMmoonnnnn . . .'

I wobbled unsteadily on the boulder, staring into the night. The pleading in my head had become hysterical, and I heard a voice moaning in a cracked whisper, as if I were listening to someone else!

'Please be there . . . you must be there . . . Oh Jesus Christ Almighty . . . Come on! I know you're there . . . help me you bastards, help me . . .'

Snowflakes feathered against my face; the wind tugged at my clothing. The night remained black. Warm tears mingled with the cold melted snow on my face. I wanted it to end. I felt destroyed. For the first time in many days I accepted that I had finally come to the end of my strength. I needed someone, anyone. This dark night-storm was taking me and I had no more will to resist. I cried for many things, but mostly for not having someone to be with in this awful night. I let my head fall to my chest, ignored the darkness, and let the anger and pain weep. It was too much for me. I just couldn't keep on; too much of everything.

'HELP MEeeeeeee!'

The howl keened out into the darkness, and the wind and snow seemed to have swallowed it the moment it was uttered.

I thought at first it was an electric flash in my head, like the sudden blinding flashes which had flared after falling into the crevasse. It didn't flash! It kept on glowing, red and green, pulsing colours into the black night. I gaped at it. Something floated and glowed ahead of me. A semicircle of red and green hanging in the night.

'A space ship? Stone me, I must be bad . . . seeing things now . . .'

Then muffled sounds, surprised sleepy sounds and brighter lights flicking out from the colours. A spray of yellow light suddenly cut out from the colours in a wide cone. More sounds, voices, not my voices, other voices.

'The tents!! They're still here . . .'

The thought paralysed me with shock. I toppled sideways off the boulder, landing in a crumpled heap on the rocky river bed. Pain surged up my thigh and I moaned. In an instant I had changed to an enfeebled, sobbing figure, incapable of

187

moving any part of my body. Something which had held me up, kept a flicker of strength pulsing, had evaporated into the storm. I tried lifting my head from the rocks to look at the lights but to no avail.

'Joe! Is that you? JOE!'

Simon's voice sounded cracked with strain. I shouted a reply but nothing came out. I was sobbing convulsively, retching from the spasmodic heavings in my chest. Incoherent words were mumbled into the dark. I turned my head to see a bobbing light approaching in a rush. There was a sound of stones rasping underfoot and someone shouting in a high-pitched voice of alarm:

'Over there, over there!'

Then the light flared over me and all I could see was the dazzle of its beam.

'Help me . . . please help.'

I felt strong arms reach round my shoulders, pulling me. Simon's face became abruptly visible.

'Joe! God! Oh my God! Fucking hell, fuck, look at you. Shit, Richard, hold him. Lift him, lift him you stupid bastard! God Joe, how? How? . . .'

Too shocked to realise what he was saying, his words tumbled out in an obscene litany, expletives said for no reason, a meaningless stream of obscenities, with Richard hovering, nervous, scared of the pain.

'Dying . . . couldn't take any more. Too much for me . . . too much . . . thought it was over . . . please help, for God's sake help me . . .'

'It'll be okay. I've got you, I have you; you're safe . . .'

Then Simon was hauling me up with his arms round my chest, dragging me, heels bumping over the rocks. Dropped heavily by the doorway of the tent in a soft glow of candlelight from within, I looked up to see Richard staring down at me, wide-eyed with apprehension. I wanted to giggle at the fuss, but tears kept crawling from my eyes and I could speak no words. Then Simon dragged me into the tent and laid me gently back against a mass of warm down sleeping bags. He knelt by my side staring at me, and I could see a confusion of pity, and horror, and alarm fighting in his eyes. I smiled at him, and he grinned back, shaking his head slowly from side to side.

'Thanks, Simon,' I said. 'You did right.' I saw him turn quickly away, averting his eyes. 'Anyway, thanks.'

He nodded silently.

The tent was full of warm light from the candle. People seemed to hover over me. Shadows played on the tent walls. An immense tiredness seemed suddenly to drain my strength. I lay still, feeling my back pressing through the soft down. Faces peered over me, two faces, constantly appearing in brief visions, confusing me. Then Richard was pressing a plastic mug into my hand.

Tea! Hot tea! But I couldn't hold it.

Simon took it from me, helped me sit up, and then fed me the tea. I saw Richard busy over the gas stove, stirring thick milky porridge, spooning sugar in as he stirred. More tea followed, and the porridge, which I couldn't eat. I stared across at Simon, seeing the haggard tension in his face and the shock in his eyes. For a moment nothing was said. With a start, I recognised the last time I had seen Simon look at me in this way. He had stood at the top of the ice cliff and stared at me for that moment too long. That instant moment when I knew he had accepted I would die. Then the spell was broken, and we burst into a torrent of questions, all blurted out at the same time, yet mostly unanswered. In that long silent meeting of eyes every question had become futile, every answer superfluous. I told him of the crevasse and the crawling. He told of his nightmare descent after the cutting and how he knew I was dead. He looked at me then as if he couldn't quite grasp that I had come back. I smiled, and touched his hand.

'Thank you,' I said again, knowing it could never tell him what I felt.

He seemed embarrassed and quickly changed the subject: 'I've burnt all your clothes!'

'What?'

'Well, I thought you weren't . . .'

189

He burst out laughing at the expression on my face, and I laughed with him. We kept at it for too long, and the sounds were harsh, almost manic.

Hours went by without us noticing, and the tent filled with a babble of voices blurting out our stories. Laughing at the money-search, and all my underwear now burnt outside the tent. Endless cups of tea given with concern, and now a deep abiding friendship. And, at every gesture, a touch on the arm, a look, an intimacy we would never have dared show before and never would again. It reminded me of those storm-swept hours on the face when for a short time we had played parts in our very own clichéd third-rate war film.

Simon forced me to finish the porridge as Richard prepared fried egg sandwiches. It seemed I swallowed a different drug with every sip of tea. Painkillers, and Ronicol, and antibiotics. I balked at the sandwiches, unable to swallow the dry bread.

'Eat it!' Simon said sternly. I coughed at the dry bread catching in my throat and mouthed it helplessly. I could get no saliva into my mouth so, despite his order, I spat it out.

'Right. Let's take a look at your leg.'

He had suddenly become stern and efficient. I started to protest but he had already begun to cut my tattered over-trousers with a penknife. I saw the blade slicing effortlessly through the thin nylon material. It was red-handled. My knife. The last time it had been used on me was three and a half days ago. A spasm of fear ran through me. I didn't want any more pain. Not today at least. Sleep was what I craved, warm downy sleep. I flinched when he raised my leg to pull the trousers away.

'It's okay. I'll be as careful as possible.'

I glanced from him to Richard, who looked as if he was going to be sick. I grinned at him, but he turned away and busied himself with the stove. I was both excited and apprehensive to see what my leg looked like. I wanted to know what had been causing me so much agony, but I was scared of seeing it rotten and infected. Simon unzipped my gaiters and gently released the laces and Velcro catches.

'Richard. You're going to have to hold his leg down. I can't pull the boot off unless you keep it firm.'

Richard hesitated by the stove. 'Can't you cut the boot off?'

'Yes, but it's unnecessary. Come on. It'll only be for a second.'

He moved to my side and held my leg gingerly below the knee. Simon began pulling at the boot and I screamed.

'Grip it tight, for Christ's sake!'

He pulled again and the pain seemed to balloon up from my knee. I squeezed my eyes shut and whimpered at the gathering flood of fire in my knee, praying for it to stop.

'Right. Got it.'

The pain ebbed quickly away. Simon threw the boot out of the tent, and Richard hurriedly let go of my leg. I think he'd had his eyes closed as well.

My polar trousers followed, sliding gently from my legs. Richard moved to the back of the tent, and I sat up expectantly. When Simon pulled my thermal long-johns off we both gawped at my leg in astonishment.

'Bloody hell!'

'Fuck me, it's enormous!'

The leg was a bloated stump stained yellow and brown, with livid purple streaks running down from the knee. There was no discernible difference between my thigh and my ankle. Only the hugely distended lump which twisted grotesquely to the right half-way down showed where the knee had been.

'God! It's worse than I thought.' I felt weak at the sight of it, and reached forward tentatively to stroke the skin around my knee. At least there was no angry inflammation, no obvious signs of infection.

'It's bad,' Simon muttered. He was examining the underside of my foot. 'You've broken your heel as well.'

'Have I? Oh well.' It didn't seem very important to me. Foot, knee, the whole caboodle, what did it matter. I was down. I could rest, and eat and sleep. It would mend.

'Yes. See those purple streaks? They're signs of haemorrhaging. You have them all round your heel, and the ankle as well.'

191

'Here you go, Richard,' I said. 'Take a look at this!'

He peered over my shoulder and then pulled away hurriedly. 'Ohhh! I wish I hadn't.'

I laughed happily, noticing how quickly I had changed. The manic hysterical laughter had become a thing of the past. Simon pulled my long-johns back over my legs with a worried expression on his face.

'We'll have to get you out of here quickly. The donkeys are coming in the morning. One of us can go down and ask Spinoza to bring a mule and his saddle as well.'

'I'll go,' Richard volunteered. 'It's half-past four now. I'll go after this tea. That way you can use my sleeping bag and Joe can take yours. I'll be back by six . . .'

'Hang on,' I interrupted. 'I need rest and food. I can't cope with two days on a mule straight away.'

'You'll just have to,' Simon said sharply. 'There's no question about it. It'll be three days at least before you get to a hospital. You've got frostbite as well as the leg, and you're exhausted. If you leave it any longer, it will get infected.'

'But –'

'Forget it! We go in the morning. It will have been broken for over a week by the time we reach Lima. You can't risk it.'

I felt too weak to argue and looked imploringly at the two of them, hoping they would change their minds. Simon ignored me and began feeding my legs into his sleeping bag. Richard passed me some tea, smiled reassuringly, and then stepped out into the night. 'Be back soon,' he shouted from the darkness, but already I was falling asleep. There seemed to be something important still to do before I slept, but I was losing the struggle to keep my eyes open. Then I remembered:

'Simon –'

'What?'

'You saved my life you know. It must have been terrible for you that night. I don't blame you. You had no choice. I understand that, and I understand why you thought I was dead. You did all that you could have done. Thanks for getting me down.'

He said nothing, and when I looked across at him lying

on his back in Richard's bag there were tears on his cheeks.
I turned away as he spoke:

'Honestly, I thought you were dead. I was sure of it . . .
couldn't see how you would possibly have survived . . .'

'It's okay. I know . . .'

'God! Coming down alone . . . Coming down, I couldn't
bear it. I mean . . . what was I going to say to your parents?
What? I'm sorry Mrs Simpson, but I had to cut the rope . . .
She'd never understand, never believe me . . .'

'It's all right. You don't have to now.'

'I wish I had stayed longer . . . just believed you could still
be alive. It would have saved you so much.'

'Doesn't matter. We're here now. It's over.'

'Yes.' He said it in a choked whisper, and I felt the
unstoppable flood of hot tears filling my eyes. How much he
had been through I could only guess at. A second later I was
asleep.

I awoke to a hubbub of voices and laughter. Girls' voices
chattered excitedly in Spanish close by the tent, and I heard
Simon talking to Richard about the donkeys. I opened my
eyes slowly to the unfamiliar glow of the tent walls. Sun
dappled the red and green fabric, and shadows passed by
every few seconds. It seemed as if there were a bazaar in full
trade outside the tent. I remembered with a shock the events
of a few hours before. I was safe; it was true. I smiled drowsily
and moved my arms against the silken downy sides of the
sleeping bag, luxuriating in the feeling of homecoming. It had
been so bad, I thought idly in half-sleep, so very bad.

An hour later I started from sleep to a voice calling my
name from far away. I felt confused. Who was calling me?
Sleep dragged me softly back to the warmth of the bag, but
the voice kept calling:

'Come on, Joe, wake up.'

I rolled my head to the side and looked blearily at the heads
crowded into the doorway. Simon knelt there with a steaming
mug of tea in his hand, and behind him the two girls peered
curiously over his shoulder. I tried to sit up but couldn't

move. A great weight was pressing down on to my chest, pinning me to the ground. I swung my arm feebly in an effort to haul myself up but it flopped limp at my side. Arms reached round my shoulders and pulled me into a sitting position:

'Drink this, and try to eat. You need it.'

I cupped the mug in my gloved hands and crouched over it, feeling the steam wetting my face. Simon moved away but the girls remained squatting near the door smiling at me. There was something unreal about them sitting there in the sun, watching me drink tea. Their wide-hipped peasant skirts and flower-strewn hats seemed very strange. What were they doing here? My mind seemed to be running off at tangents from second to second so that I couldn't fully grasp what was happening. I had got here safely. I understood the tents, and Simon and Richard, but not these weirdly dressed Peruvians. I decided that the best thing to do was ignore them and concentrate on my tea. It scalded my mouth with the first sip. The gloves which protected my frozen fingers and the lack of sensation in my hands made me forget how hot it would be. I gasped and blew quickly, trying to cool the tip of my tongue. The girls giggled.

An endless stream of food and drink followed during the next half-hour, along with quick snippets of encouragement and information about what was happening. There was some delay because Spinoza was being bloody-minded about payment for the mules. I could hear Simon's voice getting louder and more infuriated with every passing minute. I heard Richard translating calmly to Spinoza. The girls occasionally looked over at Simon and frowned. Then suddenly they were gone, and there was no more need to stay awake. I slumped forward and drifted into sleep, letting the chaotic Spanish–English row fade into the background.

A hand shook me awake again. It was Simon:

'You'll have to get out of the tent now. We're packing up. He's finally agreed on a price, and if he changes his mind again I'm going to rip his bloody head off!'

I tried to shuffle round to move out of the tent and I was horrified by how weak I had become. I fell sideways as my arm buckled beneath me when I was half out of the tent, and I couldn't push myself up again. Simon lifted me gently and dragged me clear of the sun.

'Simon, I'll never be able to cope with the mule. You don't know how weak I am.'

'It'll be all right. We'll help you.'

'Help me! I can hardly stay awake, let alone sit up. How can you help me ride a mule, for Christ's sake? I need rest. I really do. I need sleep and food. I've only had three hours' sleep since I got down . . . I . . .'

'You've got no choice. You're going today and that's that.'

I tried to protest but he was having none of it. He walked over to the tent and returned with the first-aid box. Richard passed me another mug of tea while Simon handed me my quota of pills. Then they left me and began dismantling the camp. I lay on my side watching them until I couldn't fight off the appalling drowsy weakness any longer. The deterioration scared me deeply and made me wonder anxiously whether I had burnt myself out completely. It occurred to me that I was nearer to death than when I had been alone. The minute I knew help was at hand something had collapsed inside me. Whatever had been holding me together had gone. Now I could not think for myself, let alone crawl! There was nothing to fight for, no patterns to follow, no *voice*, and it frightened me to think that, without these, I might run out of life. I tried to stay awake, fighting to shake the sleep away and keep my eyes open, but the sleep won. I dozed fitfully, waking to the babble of different languages and dozing off again to the recurrent thoughts of comas, collapse and unwaking sleep.

It seemed a long time before Simon came to me again. I heard his voice talking to Richard and looked up. He stood by my side examining me with a worried expression on his face:

'Hello. Are you all right?'

'Yes. I'm okay.' I had abandoned any idea of resisting the plan to leave.

'You don't look it. We'll be leaving soon. Perhaps it would be better if you sat up and tried to liven yourself up a bit. I'll get you some tea.'

I laughed at the thought of being livened up but managed to sit up unaided all the same. Eventually Spinoza led his old mule to me and Simon helped me to my feet. Leaning heavily on his shoulder, I hopped towards the mule, which waited patiently. It looked a pleasant-natured, calm old animal, which encouraged me. As I was about to be lifted into the saddle Richard suddenly called out:

'Hang on, Simon! We've forgotten his money.'

A hobbling search then began with Richard and Simon supporting me on either side as I directed them from rock to rock, vainly trying to remember where I had hidden the money belt. Spinoza and the girls looked puzzled. We laughed happily until at last we found the belt, and held it up for them to see. They smiled politely but clearly didn't understand what was so important about a tattered piece of tubular climbing tape.

The saddle was one of those old-style high-pommelled Western affairs with huge cups of carved leather for stirrups and ornate silver inlays round the pommel. A Karrimat had been bent over the saddle as a cushion and to keep my injured leg swinging out free from the mule's flank. We set off down the river bed at a steady walk, with Simon and Richard walking on each side of me, keeping a watchful eye on my condition.

The next two days were a blur of exhaustion and pain. I couldn't squeeze my thighs together to steer the mule, and it seemed to walk into every tree, boulder and wall that we passed in the twenty-hour journey to Cajatambo. Even with Simon spiking it with a sharpened snow stake, it still blundered on, and I screamed and howled impotently until the pain died. Somehow I managed not to fall. The familiar landscape drifted past me blurred by pain and exhaustion. At the end of each day childish tantrum feelings would rush through me. I no longer had the strength, or desperation, to cope with this added torment. I wanted it finished, wanted to get home. Simon mothered me down through the bad times, walking back and forth on the trail, goading the donkey driver to increase his pace, exhorting the man pulling my mule to take care, and walking close by my side when sleep and weakness threatened to topple me from the saddle. He took my watch from me, and halted the march every time a new drug had to be administered. Painkillers, Ronicol, antibiotics, and the inevitable tea. Tempers frayed around me as I drifted in and out of sleep while the mule walked doggedly on through high passes, steep rocky valleys and lush pampas, but Simon stayed close by my side, encouraging some faint boost of strength whenever I pleaded for a rest.

Cajatambo was a mayhem of hassle as Simon battled with the police to hire a pick-up truck, and then both he and Richard fought off the hordes of villagers trying to climb into the back for a free lift to Lima. At the last minute a young man approached the truck. I lay stretched out on a mattress in the open back. He looked sorrowfully at me, seeing the crude splint on my leg. A policeman with a machine pistol slung across his chest stepped forward and stopped Richard trying to remove the last villager from the truck.

'Señor, please for you to help this man. His legs are bad. Six days he waits. You take him to hospital . . . yes?'

There was a shocked silence as we all turned to examine the old man slumped beside me in the back of the truck. He looked imploringly at me, and then, grimacing with pain, he rolled his hips and flicked aside the crude sacking covering his legs. The crowd was suddenly deathly silent, and I heard the sharp intake of breath from Simon close by me. The man's legs were smashed. I had a brief glimpse of two distorted legs, ripped-open raw wounds, bloodstains, and the deep angry purple colour of infection. A sharp, sweet stench rose from the blanket as he replaced it gingerly over his legs.

'My God!' I felt sick.

'He is bad. Yes?'

'Bad! He hasn't a hope!'

'I'm sorry. My English is not good –'

'It's okay. We'll take him, and this man,' I interrupted.

'Thank you, Señors. You are kind men.'

The driver was an alcoholic who supplied us with generous quantities of beer. Beer, cigarettes and painkillers gave a cloudy film to my memory of those three days struggling back to Lima. Late that night we arrived at the hospital. The old man, we were told, could not afford a good hospital like this. We said it was no problem and paid the driver for the hire of the truck, with instructions to take the man to his hospital. As Richard helped me out of the truck, Simon gave the man's son our last remaining supplies of painkillers and antibiotics. The truck pulled away into a muggy hot Lima night, and from my wheelchair I saw the old man trying feebly to wave his thanks before it turned the corner of the street.

The hospital was frighteningly out-of-date by our standards, but there were clean white sheets, tinned music from the ward speakers, and pretty nurses, none of whom spoke a word of English. They wheeled me briskly down the green and white corridors, with Simon hurrying beside me unable to relinquish me from his care. The enormity of what we had been through was just beginning to sink in.

An hour later, Simon and Richard had been brusquely told to leave. After being X-rayed, my stinking climbing clothes had been taken away to be washed, and I was sat, naked, on a set of chair-scales as a pretty nurse took my pulse, noted my weight and drew a blood sample from my arm. I turned to see the scales and was horrified. Seven and a quarter stones! Three stones . . . God, I'd lost three stones! She grinned cheerfully at me before scooping me off the chair and lowering me gently into a deep bath of hot disinfected water. When she had done with me I was put to bed, and instantly fell asleep. An hour later she was back, this time with a concerned-looking doctor. He explained something frightening and complicated about my blood sample while she punctured a vein in my wrist and set up a glucose drip. I woke in the night from dreadful nightmare memories of the crevasse, soaked in sweat, and panicked to screaming point until the nurses came with words of kindness that I couldn't understand.

I lay there for two indescribable days without food, painkillers or antibiotics until my insurance was confirmed by telex and they deigned to operate on me. They came for me early in the morning. A pre-med injection in my arm an hour earlier had reduced me to a familiar enfeebled, barely conscious state. Two people, masked, wearing green, muttered unintelligibly at me as they wheeled me down seemingly endless tiled corridors. It wasn't until we neared the operating theatre that the fear in my stomach rose up as panic. I mustn't go through with this! Must stop them. Wait until you get home, for the love of God, don't let them do it.

'I don't want the operation.'

I said it calmly. I thought that I had said it clearly, but they did not answer. Perhaps the drug has affected my speech? I repeated the sentence. One of them nodded at me, but they didn't stop. Then it hit me. They don't understand English. I tried to sit up but someone pushed me back on to the pillows. I shouted, panic-stricken, for them to stop. The trolley clattered through the swing doors of the operating theatre. A man spoke to me in Spanish. His voice was melodic. He was trying to calm me, but the sight of him checking a syringe made me struggle to a half-sitting position.

'Please. I don't –'

A strong hand pressed me back. Another gripped my arm and I felt the slight pain of the needle. I tried to lift my head but somehow it had doubled in weight. Turning to the side I saw a tray of instruments. Above me bright lights came on, and the room began to swim before my eyes. I had to say something . . . had to stop them. Darkness slipped over the lights and slowly all sounds muffled down to silence.

POSTSCRIPT

June 1987. Hunza Valley, Karakoram Himalayas, Pakistan

I watched the two small figures gradually dwindle into invisibility on the bleak hillside above me. Andy and Jon were going for the summit of the unclimbed 20,000-foot Tupodam. I was alone again in the mountains, but I had chosen to be.

I turned away and tended the little gas stove heating my second cup of coffee. The movement made my knee ache. I swore irritably and leant forward to massage the pain away. Arthritis. The scars of six operations stood out lividly on the distorted joint. At least the wounds in my mind had healed better than these.

The doctors had told me I would get arthritis. They had said the whole knee-joint would have to be removed within the next ten years: but then they had said a lot of things, few of which were true. 'You will never bend the knee again, Mr Simpson . . . You will have a permanent limp. You'll never climb again . . .'

They were right about the arthritis, though, I thought ruefully as I turned off the stove and glanced anxiously back to the hillside. The first sharp stab of fear for them tremored through me. Come back safe. At least do that, I whispered to the now silent hills. Given fine weather they should be down in three days. I knew it would be a long wait.

I felt sad to have dropped out of the summit attempt. The leg had worked so well, but then the pain had started. I knew that to climb here only ten weeks after the last operation was inviting fresh injury but I was glad I had tried, and there was always next year.

201

Six days earlier we had reached the col beneath the shoulder of our mountain, and dug a snow cave. We had sat outside gazing silently at the Himalayas stretching away from us. The sun had burnt down from an endless blue sky, and the sea of snow summits was etched sharply in the crystal clear air. This was what I had come to see. Pristine, untouchable. Lofting into the sky, perfectly beautiful. The sun glittered diamanté reflections off frozen snow crystals. Karun Koh loomed above, only five miles distant. I fancied I could see the curve of the earth in the limitless horizon of peaks set before me. I tried to believe I could see Everest despite knowing it was 1,000 miles from here. The names of the ranges rolled through my mind: the Hindu Kush, the Pamirs, Tibet and the Karakorams. Everest, goddess mother of the snows, Nanda Devi, K2, Nanga Parbat, Kanchenjunga; so much history in those names. And of all those who had climbed on them. Suddenly they were real to me, as they never would have been had I chosen not to return. Somewhere out in those serried peaks lay the bodies of two of my friends, alone, buried in the snows on different mountains. That was the dark side of this beauty which for this moment, I could close from my mind.

I packed my rucksack, shouldered it and, after one last look towards where they had disappeared, turned away and began the walk back to camp.

Ten Years On . . .

In his book about another climb in the Andes, *Against the Wall* (published in 1997), Simon Yates was kind enough to acknowledge that I had told his side of the Siula Grande story 'faithfully and truly' in *Touching the Void*, and he ruminated on the questions of conscience that might have remained a decade or so after the event. I am so relieved to hear him say that his conscience is clear, for he did what I would have done in his place, the only sensible course open to him at the end of an heroic attempt to rescue me. He wrote:

> Some would argue that there was no decision to be made; that cutting the rope and the powerful symbol of trust and friendship it represents should never have entered my mind. Others say that it was simply a matter of survival, something I was forced to do.
>
> As it happened, for a long time I simply hung on, hoping that Joe would be able to take his weight off the rope and relieve my position. By the time I remembered I had a knife in the top of my rucsac I was at the end of my tether, unable to hold him for much longer. I knew I had done all that could reasonably be expected of me to save Joe, and now both our lives were being threatened, I had reached a point where I had to look after myself. Although I knew my action might result in his death, I took the decision intuitively in a split second. It simply felt the right thing to do, like so many critical decisions I had taken during the climb. Without hesitation, I

removed the knife from the rucsac and cut the rope.

Such moments of intuition always seem to feel the same – impersonal, as if the decision has not come from my own mind. Only with hindsight could I see there had been a build-up to that moment. During the days before, we had made many errors of judgement. We had not eaten or drunk enough and carried on climbing long after nightfall. By doing so, we had allowed ourselves to become cold, exhausted and dehydrated. One evening I became so cold waiting outside for Joe to finish digging a snow-hole that some of my fingers became frostbitten. In short, we had not looked after ourselves . . .

I can see now that Simon is right, though I didn't always view it this way, as a matter of neglect.

Analysing after a climb what you did correctly or incorrectly is as important as being fit or talented. So it was natural that for several years I too mulled over what had happened and tried to work out where we had gone wrong and what vital mistakes we had made. At first I was convinced we had done nothing wrong. I would still have back-climbed the ice cliff in the way I did, although perhaps with a little more care about the quality of the ice. We would still have climbed Alpine-style, used snow-caves instead of tents and carried the same equipment and food. It was Simon who eventually pointed out to me where we had made our fatal mistake, and it happened before we left base camp.

Gas.

We hadn't allowed ourselves enough gas to keep us adequately hydrated. One small canister between the two of us per day was simply insufficient. So as to save weight, we had pared everything down to the minimum. It left us no room to manoeuvre when things started to go so drastically wrong. When Simon lowered me to near the Santa Rosa col, and before we committed ourselves to descending the West Face in a gathering storm and imminent darkness, we had considered digging a snow-cave and sitting the storm out. If we had done that we could have made the lowers on a bright and sunny day. We would have seen and avoided the ice cliff, and remained in control.

Instead, as the storm cloud gathered over the col, we were painfully aware that we had run out of food and gas the previous night. Already dangerously dehydrated, we couldn't risk the possibility of being trapped by a prolonged storm with no way of producing fluid. I was already suffering the dehydrating and weakening effect of a traumatic fracture of a major bone and the consequent internal bleeding. We had no choice. For the sake of a canister of gas to melt ice and snow for warm drinks, we had to carry on. And so we lost control, and nearly our lives.

In his book Simon continues his analysis:

All my agonising after cutting the rope had not changed anything. My decision had been right; we had both survived. In subsequent years, I have overheard numerous heated debates about the ethics of my decision and many 'what if' scenarios. I have met people who are understanding of my actions and others who are openly hostile. Their secondhand opinions mean nothing compared to the words Joe uttered to me in the tent that night in Peru. With the greater mountaineering skills and experience I now possess, I do not believe that I would get into such a situation again, but if somehow I did, I know that my decision would be the same. In just one respect I feel I was neglectful. In the extreme stress of my predicament I came to the conclusion without a close inspection that any attempt at rescue in the crevasse was impossible. On reflection, I can see that it would probably have done more harm than good to have tried, but it simply did not occur to me to go to the edge and look carefully into the depths.

Ultimately, we all have to look after ourselves, whether on mountains or in day to day life. In my view that is not a licence to be selfish, for only by taking good care of ourselves are we able to help others. Away from the mountains, in the complexity of everyday life, the price of neglecting this responsibility might be a marriage breaking down, a disruptive child, a business failing or a house repossessed. In the mountains the penalty for neglect can often be death.

'Secondhand opinions', as Simon puts it, were never something I paid much attention to after the accident. We knew exactly what had happened between us and were quite happy with it. I wrote this book in the hope that, by telling the story 'straight', it might nip in the bud any harsh or unfair criticism of Simon. The rope cutting had clearly touched a nerve, transgressed some unwritten rule, and people seemed to be drawn to that element of the story – until I wrote it down as honestly as I could.

Even so, the misinformed opinions of some armchair adventurers were never going to worry either of us for long. Recovering from my injuries and getting back to the mountains were my priorities, not vague speculation by others on what we should or should not have done. Ninety per cent of accidents are down to human error. We are fallible, and accidents will happen. I suppose the trick is to anticipate all the possible consequences of what you set out to do so that, if things do go wrong, you are better able to stay in control.

I can add only that however painful readers may think our experiences were, for me this book still falls short of articulating just how dreadful were some of those lonely days. I simply could not find the words to express the utter desolation of the experience.

Joe Simpson
August 1997

Epilogue
BAD MEMORIES

In mid-July 2002 I stood at the precise point where seventeen years earlier Simon Yates had found me on a dark snow-filled night in the Peruvian Andes. At that time I had been an emotionally and physically shattered wreck of a human being. I weighed a little under ninety pounds, was suffering from keto-acidosis and was close to falling into a coma. My body was as near to total exhaustion as it is possible to get without dying. I suspect now, having spoken to a number of doctors, that I probably was dying when Simon found me that night.

Now, all these years later, I was uncomfortably aware of the camera man, the director and the sound man watching expectantly as they pointed a lens and a long furry microphone at me. Simon was standing by my side explaining to the camera what it had been like to find me, the state I was in, and the way I was lying on the rocks.

I seemed to be hearing all this from a distance. I could feel that my heart-rate was increasing rapidly and I was acutely conscious of the surrounding mountains. They seemed to press in on me. I felt out of breath. A hot flush ran through me and I started sweating copiously. I shifted uncomfortably hoping the camera was not picking up on these signs.

I was feeling strangely vulnerable as if about to be attacked. In fact the more I thought about it the more worried I became. I was asked a question and I seemed to be hearing it from a long way away. I could hear the blood pumping in my temples. As I started speaking I was trying furiously not to cry. I had been determined not to give a teary interview and yet now I was being ambushed. I heard myself talking about the moment Simon and Richard came looking for me in the dark, the sight of their head torches and that exquisite moment when I realised the nightmare was over and that the rest of my life had just been given back to me.

I looked down at the ground where I had been found lying face down on the rocks and then glanced up the river bed of chaotic jumbled boulders. *How on earth did I get down that in the dark?*

The thought seemed to make the feelings of panic stronger. I'm not even sure whether I stopped talking but for a long moment as I looked at the ground I had the feeling of lying there, the uncanny sensation of Simon's hands gripping me by the shoulders and rolling me over and holding me. I almost turned around to see who had touched my shoulders.

It was as if something hallucinogenic had happened to my brain; synapses had crossed, colours, feelings and sensation from some long deep hidden memory had come bursting back with a quite shocking force. Perhaps it lasted a millisecond. It seemed like minutes. Then the moment was gone and I was left feeling completely unnerved.

Simon and I walked back towards where the film crew had reconstructed our original base camp. It looked very familiar. I think Simon must have noticed something. He asked if I was okay. I said, 'No, not really,' and not much more. I wanted to run away. I sat down and tried to calm myself. Externally I appeared quite normal. Inside I was feeling hysterical.

Back in the huge base camp twenty minutes' walk down the valley I began to feel a little better. I went to my tent, poured a shot of whisky into a tin mug, lit a cigarette, and thought. *'Joe, that was a panic attack. Don't worry, it's normal.'*

In truth I don't know what it was but it was to happen repeatedly over the next three weeks, perhaps not so strongly, but that may have been because I was bracing myself for the attacks. Telling myself as they came on that it was just my mind playing tricks on me and that it would fade helped.

As we had made the slow four-day walk-in to the camp with a fourteen-strong group comprising the film crew, the safety team, porters and seventy-six donkeys, I hadn't the slightest anxiety about being back in that familiar landscape. In fact it all seemed farcical. Dressing up in '80s style gear and re-enacting the approach with four recalcitrant donkeys and the team doctor disguised as Richard Hawking was a combination of hilarious farce and tedious repetition. We tramped past the camera tripod then scurried around, herding the confused *burros* back the way they had come so we could do yet another take.

'Start walking for camera when you get to the large patch of lupins.' This cryptic instruction squawked from the radio and we glanced at the distant notch on the ridge where the camera with the big 600mm lens fitted was set up. We then examined the steeply angled walls of the v-shaped valley which we are about to traverse. The slopes ran thousands of feet down from a jagged rocky ridge line to the thin glinting sinuous lines of a river far below us. The entire hillside was covered in lupins.

When I sighted the snow-covered peaks as we rounded the valley far above the village of Huayllapa I registered only pleasant surprise to see old friends again. The ice-sheathed peaks of Rasac and Yerupaja dominated the head of the valley. My reaction was one of interest rather than foreboding. I had forgotten how beautiful these mountains were and realised with a start that despite twenty years of climbing mountains all over the world the Cordillera Huayhuash was still the most beautiful mountain range I have ever laid my eyes upon. It made me smile.

Then I saw the West face of Siula Grande and felt a tremor of fear. It was bigger and meaner and so much more threatening than I remembered. It made me wonder at the person I had been all those years ago. I must have been bold, ambitious or even a little crazy to have considered such an undertaking. I traced the line of our ascent and watched the snow pluming off the north ridge in the strong high-altitude winds. It scared me. Where had all that drive and passion gone? How had I lost that sense of invincibility, the confidence born of youth, too much testosterone and too little imagination?

As I turned from the face and trudged up the jumbled moraine fields on the glacier I consoled myself with the thought that at least I was here; a little greyer round the temples, only a little wiser, but at least I was here.

The days spent re-enacting for the camera the crawling on the glacier and the moraines were both surreal and disturbing. I knew everything was being filmed so that my face could not be recognised when they cut the film in with action reconstructions filmed with actors in the Alps. Nevertheless it felt irritating to have to go through the unnerving business of dressing up in the same mountaineering clothing, wrapping the yellow foam mat around my right leg and then pretending to crawl and fall and hop as I had done seventeen years earlier. *Why couldn't they have just used an actor out here?* I kept asking myself.

I felt as if I was about to be attacked from behind at any moment. The feelings became most powerful when I was on the moraines or the glacier and the familiar cirque of mountain ridges dominated my every view. It was a memory that had been seared into my consciousness. Seeing it again all these years later was the trigger that brought back my worst memories and associations. This was the place where I had known I was going to die. Those ridge lines should have been the last thing I would ever see. I should never have come back. It was not cathartic. It was terrifying.

Oddly enough Simon and I hardly spoke to each other about our personal feelings. So much had been written and spoken about the experience it was as if there was no more to be said and therefore no point speaking about it. Nothing would change. In our hearts we knew better than anyone what had happened in this place. It was history and we had dealt with it.

For me the memories came rushing back with such a clarity and startling vividness that I became convinced at times that the last seventeen years had not passed by and I was back in the terrible reality of 1985 trying to crawl down the mountain.

One day I was alone in a narrow sandy gulch running between the moraines and the valley walls. I sat staring at the miles of jumbled rocks with my leg strapped and the clothes and rucksacks donned waiting for the radio call from the film crew perched on a high ridge over a mile away. Again I began to panic. In 1985 I had sat in this precise spot convinced that Simon and Richard were following along behind me. That had been an hallucination, a cocoon of comfort I had hidden in so well that I had believed it completely. It was no weirder than the one that I now seemed to be experiencing seventeen years later.

I kept peering nervously over my shoulder trying to make out the people on the ridge. My heart began racing and I kept sucking in deep nervous breaths. I thought I might burst into tears. Then I spotted the tiny figures huddled around the camera and tried to calm myself. The sense of menace increased when I heard the rattle of rocks tumbling down the valley walls and spurts of dust drifted away on the wind. They were uncomfortably close. I glanced back at the ridge. *Come on, come on. I want to get out of here.* Another volley of rocks spat down towards me. I jerked away instinctively. Seconds later a feeling of all-consuming panic overwhelmed me. I had to run from the place, had to escape. Just as I began to remove the mat strapped to my leg the radio squawked into life.

'Joe, this is Kevin, do you copy?' I stared at the radio aerial poking from my chest pocket. 'Joe, Joe, do you copy? Are you ready for the take?'

'Kevin, this is Joe. I copy,' I released the transmit button and let out a long sigh of relief.

'Okay, Joe, begin to crawl towards the rocky narrows please. In your own time.' I began to laugh. It had a slightly manic edge. I was not enjoying my return to Peru.

*

Traumatic emotions; feelings of guilt, regret, sadness and terror travel hard-wired neural pathways in a manner that mimics ingrained or archetypal fears. There have been huge advances into the shadows of memory and deep-seated fear. Today scientists are discovering ways to help the brain unlearn fears and inhibitions. Tests on mice and rats have shown that the brain's hormonal reactions to such memories can be inhibited thereby softening the emotions that they evoke. In short they are mastering the means of short-circuiting the very wiring of primal fear in the mind. The source of your worst nightmares, real or imagined terrors, radiates from a dense knot of neurons called the amygdala. With each new traumatic experience, or the reliving of an old one, this 'fear centre' triggers a release of hormones that sear horrifying impressions on your brain. The unbearable becomes unforgettable. The research is aimed at helping victims fend off the ravages of post-traumatic stress disorder. The first human trials with betablocker propranolol have already taken place in America. For the medicine to be effective patients have to take them as soon after the event as possible.

I had always been a little sceptical about the very idea of post-traumatic stress disorder. It seems that everyone gets it nowadays and I was suspicious that it had become a catchall to provide exculpation from the past and a convenient way of suing for compensation. Why were not millions of people paralysed by post-traumatic stress disorders after the first and second world wars, both soldiers and civilians alike who bore witness to the most appalling experiences imaginable on a scale never before encountered? Certainly by the Second World War 'shell-shock' had been recognised as something other than 'lacking moral fibre'. Perhaps the difference then was that people did not live in the ghastly blame and compensation culture that we do today.

So it came as some surprise to be told on my return from Peru that I was suffering from post-traumatic stress disorder. In all likelihood the memory of the mountains surrounding the moraines and glacier had been so powerfully ingrained that it had brought the fears of 1985 back to me with quite startling lucidity. It was as if it had happened a few days before.

I was told that the effect would soon wear off since I seemed to have dealt so effectively with the traumas of Siula Grande in the intervening seventeen years. I was put on a waiting list for an appointment with a psychotherapist, which was something that I was deeply uncomfortable about. I had always felt a certain disdain, bordering on contempt, for the particularly American reliance on therapy and counselling. The very British 'stiff upper lip' approach to such matters seemed the most effective and most dignified remedy. However, I had to admit to feeling pretty strange on my return so I reluctantly agreed to the appointment.

In the meantime I experienced eight weeks of mild panic attacks, a tendency to cry unexpectedly and a persistent feeling of vulnerability. Then I gave a corporate motivational presentation recounting the 'Void' story and within days the symptoms had disappeared. It took six months before someone rang me about a possible appointment. I declined the offer with a few choice words about the parlous state of the health service and felt relieved that I hadn't been suffering from a serious mental illness.

Telling and retelling the 'Void' story had inadvertently proved to be a good treatment for the condition. Apparently it is common practice for psychotherapists to make a victim recount as vividly as they can the full horrors of their experience. With each telling of their real story it gradually becomes a fiction, becomes someone else's experience, and they can separate themselves from the trauma. In short the hard-wired neural pathways to the amygdala, the fear centre, are blocked or at very least by-passed.

When I went to see one of the first screenings of the drama documentary at a theatre in Soho I was filled with mixed emotions. I was relieved that it was all over and something had at last been made after more than ten years of negotiating movie deals for the rights of the book. At one point it had been sold to a combined production company involving Sally Field and Tom Cruise. It was meant to be a 'star vehicle' for Cruise which caused general hilarity in the climbing world and many jokes about Nicole Kidman playing the part of Simon. I knew at the time that if the film were ever made it would be the usual tripe that the Hollywood studios serve up each year. They were however paying an awful lot of money to make tripe. When the deal fell through and the rights reverted to me I was pleased to hear that a respected drama documentary company, Darlow Smithson, were interested in the rights. With Kevin Macdonald, an Oscar award-winning drama documentary director, on board, I had hopes that maybe a respectable film of the book might be made.

By the time I entered the theatre I had no idea what it was going to be like. Apart from my own personal difficulties in Peru the whole business of film making had proved to be both staggeringly tedious and utterly confusing. I was painfully aware of how easy it would be to make a complete mess filming the book.

One hour and forty minutes later I sat in my seat as the credits rolled feeling pleased and anxious. The film was remarkably faithful to the book and although I am the last person to judge it I felt it was a powerful and emotional production. I was anxious because I had not realised how exposed Simon and I would be until I saw the way we narrated the entire story to camera. Neither of us had ever sought that sort of public exposure and it made for uncomfortable viewing. If hearing a recording of your own voice feels odd, seeing yourself on a big screen is downright disturbing! It is always difficult to make a satisfactory film of a popular book but in this case they seem to have succeeded. That, however, is for readers and viewers to judge. The real experience, of which I had been so powerfully reminded, would always distance Simon and me from any written or celluloid representation.

Oddly enough the physical and emotional trauma experienced in Peru in 1985 did not change my life. It was the success of *Touching the Void* and my future writing and speaking career that materially changed me. The making of the film will no doubt bring further changes and challenges.

I often wonder what would have happened to my life if we had not had the accident on Siula Grande. A part of me thinks that I would have gone on to climb harder and harder routes taking greater risks each time. Given the toll of friends over the years I'm not confident that I would be alive today. In

214

those days I was a penniless, narrow-minded, anarchic, abrasive and ambitious mountaineer. The accident opened up a whole new world for me. Without it I would never have discovered hidden talents for writing and public speaking. Despite having worked hard I do sometimes wonder whether I just got lucky?

In Peru we had gone to unusual lengths to take the ultimate risk and yet despite all the pain and trauma it now seems a small price to pay for such an inspiring adventure. Isn't memory a wonderful deceiver? Almost losing everything in Peru was a sensation quite as life-enhancing as winning. I seem to have been on a worryingly long winning streak ever since. Where will it all end?

It is a hot sunny day in Sheffield as I struggle to write my seventh book, a novel. I'm trying not to be distracted by a forthcoming fly fishing holiday in Ireland followed by a fourth attempt on the North Face of the Eiger. A busy autumn of speaking engagements and publicity for the release of the film beckons. Fighting for my life on Siula Grande seventeen years ago seems to have turned me into a successful businessman, which is very odd . . .

Life can deal you an amazing hand. Do you play it steady, bluff like crazy or go all in? I'll never know.

Joe Simpson
July 2003

ACKNOWLEDGMENTS

In writing this book I felt I was taking a gamble with the odds
stacked against me. Without the support and encouragement
of friends and relatives I would never have started, let alone
finished.

Apart from so much that I already owe Simon, I must first
express my gratitude for his honesty in telling me how much
he had been through, and his trust in allowing me to write
these sensitive emotions in my own words.

Then Jim Perrin's early advice, and Geoff Birtle's encouragement by publishing my articles in *High* magazine, were
especially appreciated. Tony Colwell, my editor at Cape, gave
me invaluable help and advice, and without his conviction that
the story was worthy of a book, all would have come to
nought. I am also indebted to Jon Stevenson for prodding me
into action.

Thanks also go to Tom Richardson for the drawings, to Ian
Smith who helped me with the photographs, and to Bernard
Newman of *Mountain* magazine for rescuing most of my
slides which had been badly abused by other magazines and
newspapers. Without the generous financial support of the
Porchester Group Insurance Services, and in particular Gary
Deaves, Simon and I would have been unable to go to Peru in
the first place.

Lastly, and most important, I wish to thank my parents for
encouraging me to write the book, helping me get my mind
and body back to normal, and patiently accepting my decision
to continue climbing.

JOE SIMPSON
Storms of Silence

'To mix a metaphor, Joe Simpson is a streetwise mountaineer
. . . He takes you close to the nitty-gritty, the nuts and bolts
of professionally climbing in the 1990s. He is used to dealing
with totalitarian policemen. He is passionate and moving on
the subject of Tibet and the agonies inflicted on it by the cruel
Chinese occupation . . . Above all, Simpson is a born writer'
Paul Johnson, *The Times*

'This book's major theme is the nature of aggression. A skin-
head in a Sheffield bar sets the reader up for the genocide that
is modern Tibetan history . . . What makes Joe Simpson stand
out is his belief that there is more to life than a crampon, and
his dogged refusal to leave the highest mental peaks unclimbed'
Sara Wheeler, *Daily Telegraph*

'This immensely accessible book offers a unique re-
interpretation of masculinity . . . In doing so, it offers a
ray of hope to an increasingly bleak and vicious society'
Martin Booth, *Independent*

VINTAGE BOOKS
London

JOE SIMPSON

This Game of Ghosts

The Sequel to *Touching the Void*

'*This Game of Ghosts* is a strange, beautiful, bewildering and often very moving book . . . Simpson paints a warm, vivid picture of the climbing fraternity, and approaches a fusion of poetry and philosophy sometimes with his descriptions of the impact on oneself of facing down the fear of dying; through this coming closer to understanding death, and thereby, joyously, life'

The List

'This book is Simpson's rehabilitation. It's deeply honest, perplexed, confused, has no easy conclusions . . . This is not so much another climbing book as a psychological document, terrifying, challenging and extraordinary'

Scotsman

'This is a remarkable book by a remarkably lucky individual, a homage to a breed of men and women who to the rest of us may appear to be touched by lunacy, but who are forever questioning, forever valiant'

Sunday Express

VINTAGE BOOKS
London

THE HISTORY OF VINTAGE

The famous American publisher Alfred A. Knopf (1892–1984) founded Vintage Books in the United States in 1954 as a paperback home for the authors published by his company. Vintage was launched in the United Kingdom in 1990 and works independently from the American imprint although both are part of the international publishing group, Random House.

Vintage in the United Kingdom was initially created to publish paperback editions of books acquired by the prestigious hardback imprints in the Random House Group such as Jonathan Cape, Chatto & Windus, Hutchinson and later William Heinemann, Secker & Warburg and The Harvill Press. There are many Booker and Nobel Prize-winning authors on the Vintage list and the imprint publishes a huge variety of fiction and non-fiction. Over the years Vintage has expanded and the list now includes great authors of the past – who are published under the Vintage Classics imprint – as well as many of the most influential authors of the present.

For a full list of the books Vintage publishes, please visit our website
www.vintage-books.co.uk

For book details and other information about the classic authors we publish, please visit the Vintage Classics website
www.vintage-classics.info